1000 GREETINGS MORE

ROCKPORT

DESIGN

AESTHETIC MOVEMENT
WWW.AESTHETICMOVEMENT.COM

FONTS

AAUX PRO, ARCHER, CLARENDON, CYCLONE, LUBALIN, ZEBRAWOOD

First published in the United States of America by
Rockport Publishers, a member of Quayside Publishing Group
100 Cummings Ccenter
Suite 406-L
Beverly, Massachusetts 01915-6101
Telephone: (978) 282-9590
Fax: (978) 283-2742
www.rockpub.com

ISBN-13: 978-1-59253-640-5
ISBN-10: 1-59253-640-9

10 9 8 7 6 5 4 3 2 1

Printed in China

1000 MORE GREETINGS

CREATIVE CORRESPONDENCE FOR ALL OCCASIONS

AESTHETIC **A/M** MOVEMENT

BEVERLY MASSACHUSETTS

ROCKPORT PUBLISHERS

GREETINGS & SALUTATIONS,

In this age of eblasts, evites, and ecards, an actual physical greeting is becoming increasingly rare and ever more special. In reviewing the numerous entries that came through our studio, we made a conscious decision to omit digital forms of communication for this edition, choosing instead to focus on printed pieces. This is not to imply that a digital greeting can't look appealing and serve a purpose, but printed pieces do more than just deliver a message—in the most successful instances they become keepsakes, tokens to commemorate the events and special occasions throughout one's life.

As our society becomes more visually savvy and discerning, designers are challenged to create pieces that will grab the viewer's attention and stand apart. Tapping into their arsenal of tools, designers are employing original imagery, witty copy, unexpected materials, and unique printing techniques to enhance their work.

Since the original *1,000 Greetings* book was published in 2004, we've noticed an even greater shift toward mediums and production techniques that highlight the artisanal, skillfully assembled with a concrete knowledge of design and typography. The result is a well-balanced aesthetic between craft and design that is being created and articulated. Another thing we noticed while editing the work was the incredibly large number of submissions from independent vendors. With online marketplace resources such as Etsy, Cafepress, and Zazzle, individuals and small companies are now able to conveniently produce and sell paper goods to a large, global market. Lastly, a large majority of the work submitted utilized environmentally conscious recycled paper, which is consistent with the general attitude shared by the design community at large.

1,000 More Greetings highlights a diverse cross section of current trends in graphic design. Corporate cutbacks and increased electronic connectivity are each variables that have contributed to the democratization of design, in this past year especially, and the collection on view in this book is a reflection of that. Everything from mass-produced to limited-edition pieces, from hand-drawn to computer-generated art, from conventional to renegade printing methods are all represented side-by-side in this compilation.

We at Aesthetic Movement support the continued creation of printed matter and encourage the exchange of personal correspondence.

WITH HEARTFELT SINCERITY,

Aesthetic Movement

01 GREETING CARDS

0001–0002 : **BLANCA GÓMEZ/COSAS MINIMAS** : SPAIN

0003 : **ORANGEBEAUTIFUL** : USA

0004 : **ORANGEBEAUTIFUL** : USA

0005 : **ORANGEBEAUTIFUL** : USA

0006 : **ORANGEBEAUTIFUL** : USA

0007 : **OH JOY!** : USA

0008 : **OH JOY!** : USA

0009 : **OH JOY!** : USA

0010 : **OH JOY!** : USA

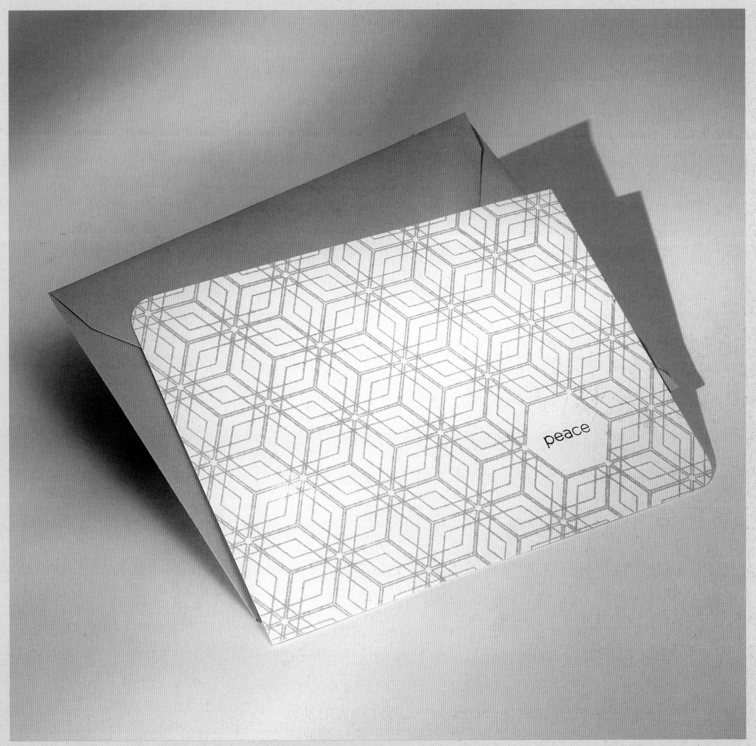

Greetings!

0012 : **SELTZER, LLC** : USA

0013 : **SCREECH OWL DESIGN** : USA

0014 : **SCREECH OWL DESIGN** : USA

Life is messy. Wear a smock!

0015 : **SELTZER, LLC** : USA

0016 : **SCREECH OWL DESIGN** : USA

0017 : **SCREECH OWL DESIGN** : USA

0018 : **SCREECH OWL DESIGN** : USA

0019 : **SELTZER, LLC** : USA

0020 : **SELTZER, LLC** : USA

0021 : **SELTZER, LLC** : USA

0022 : **LA FAMILIA GREEN** : USA

0023 : **LA FAMILIA GREEN** : USA

0024 : **ART SCHOOL GIRL** : USA

0025 : **LA FAMILIA GREEN** : USA

Thank You.

0026 : **CRACKED DESIGNS LLC** : USA

If you can't fix it with duct tape or a martini it ain't worth fixing.

0027 : **SELTZER, LLC** : USA

PART MAN. PART MACHINE.

0028 : **HULDRA PRESS** : USA

Moms Everywhere Pray for a "Good Hair Day".

0029 : **SELTZER, LLC** : USA

IF WE WERE ACTORS FILMING A LOVE SCENE I'D MAKE A SMALL MISTAKE SO WE'D HAVE TO TRY AGAIN.

0031 : **BOB'S YOUR UNCLE** : USA

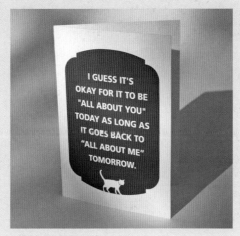

0032 : **SELTZER, LLC** : USA

0033 : **BOB'S YOUR UNCLE** : USA

0034 : **SELTZER, LLC** : USA

0035 : **BOB'S YOUR UNCLE** : USA

0036 : **SELTZER, LLC** : USA

0037 : **BOB'S YOUR UNCLE** : USA

0038 : **SELTZER, LLC** : USA

0039 : **BOB'S YOUR UNCLE** : USA

0040 : BOB'S YOUR UNCLE : USA

0041 : BOB'S YOUR UNCLE : USA

0042 : BOB'S YOUR UNCLE : USA

0044 : BOB'S YOUR UNCLE : USA

0043 : BOB'S YOUR UNCLE : USA

0045 : BOB'S YOUR UNCLE : USA

0046 : **BOB'S YOUR UNCLE** : USA

0047 : **BOB'S YOUR UNCLE** : USA

0048 : **BOB'S YOUR UNCLE** : USA

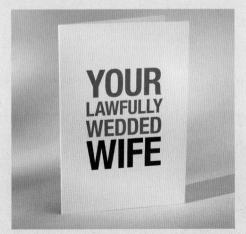

0049 : **BOB'S YOUR UNCLE** : USA

0050 : **BOB'S YOUR UNCLE** : USA

0051 : **BOB'S YOUR UNCLE** : USA

0052 : BOB'S YOUR UNCLE : USA

0053 : BOB'S YOUR UNCLE : USA

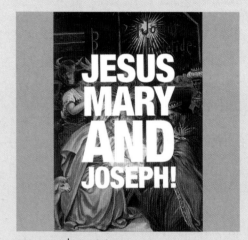

0054 : BOB'S YOUR UNCLE : USA

0055 : BOB'S YOUR UNCLE : USA

0056 : BOB'S YOUR UNCLE : USA

0057 : BOB'S YOUR UNCLE : USA

WISHING YOU A VERY Merry Christmas AND AN AWESOME NEW YEAR

0059 : **RUTH HUIMERIND** : ESTONIA

0060 : **CLAUDIA PEARSON ILLUSTRATION** : USA

0061 : **RIFLE PAPER CO.** : USA

0062 : **RIFLE PAPER CO.** : USA

0063 : **DESIGN DES TROY** : USA

0064 : **ART SCHOOL GIRL** : USA

0065 : **PUP & PONY PRESS** : USA

0066 : **ART SCHOOL GIRL** : USA

0067 : **PUP & PONY PRESS** : USA

0075 : **RUBY VICTORIA LETTERPRESS + PRINTMAKING** : AUSTRALIA

0076–0078 : **AUSTIN PRESS** : USA

0079 : **AUSTIN PRESS** : USA

0080 : **RUBY VICTORIA LETTERPRESS + PRINTMAKING** : AUSTRALIA

I WOULD TRADE TWO OF MY OTHER FRIENDS FOR YOU

0082 : **SYCAMORE STREET PRESS** : USA

happy birthday

0083 : **SYCAMORE STREET PRESS** : USA

je t'aime.

0084 : **SYCAMORE STREET PRESS** : USA

i'm sorry

0085 : **SYCAMORE STREET PRESS** : USA

0086 : **ANDY PRATT DESIGN** : USA

0087 : **ANDY PRATT DESIGN** : USA

0088 : **ANDY PRATT DESIGN** : USA

0089 : **ANDY PRATT DESIGN** : USA

0090 : **POP + SHORTY** : USA

0091 : **CLAUDIA PEARSON ILLUSTRATION** : USA

0092–0094 : **ELEVATED PRESS** : USA

0095 : **BLANCA GÓMEZ/COSAS MINIMAS** : SPAIN

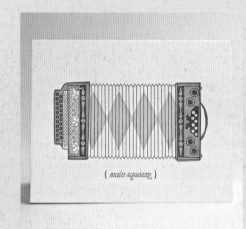

0096 : **ELEVATED PRESS** : USA

0097 : **CLAUDIA PEARSON ILLUSTRATION** : USA

0098 : **ORANGEBEAUTIFUL** : USA

0099 : **CLAUDIA PEARSON ILLUSTRATION** : USA

0100 : **ELEVATED PRESS** : USA

0101 : **ANDY PRATT DESIGN** : USA

0102 : **ANDY PRATT DESIGN** : USA

0103 : **ANDY PRATT DESIGN** : USA

0104 : **ANDY PRATT DESIGN** : USA

0105 : **ANDY PRATT DESIGN** : USA

0106 : **ANDY PRATT DESIGN** : USA

0107 : **ANDY PRATT DESIGN** : USA

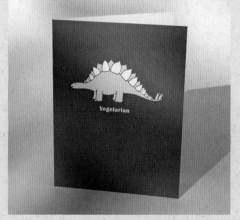

0108 : **ANDY PRATT DESIGN** : USA

0109 : **ANDY PRATT DESIGN** : USA

0110 : **DARLING CLEMENTINE** : NORWAY

0111 : **DARLING CLEMENTINE** : NORWAY

0112 : **DARLING CLEMENTINE** : NORWAY

0113 : **DARLING CLEMENTINE** : NORWAY

0114 : **DARLING CLEMENTINE** : NORWAY

0115 : **DARLING CLEMENTINE** : NORWAY

0116 : **ART SCHOOL GIRL** : USA

0117 : **ART SCHOOL GIRL** : USA

0119 : **DARLING CLEMENTINE** : NORWAY

0118 : **DARLING CLEMENTINE** : NORWAY

0120 : **DARLING CLEMENTINE** : NORWAY

0121 : **DARLING CLEMENTINE** : NORWAY

0122 : **DARLING CLEMENTINE** : NORWAY

0123 : **DARLING CLEMENTINE** : NORWAY

0124 : **DARLING CLEMENTINE** : NORWAY

0125 : **DARLING CLEMENTINE** : NORWAY

0126 : **DARLING CLEMENTINE** : NORWAY

0127 : **DARLING CLEMENTINE** : NORWAY

0128 : **DARLING CLEMENTINE** : NORWAY

0129 : **DARLING CLEMENTINE** : NORWAY

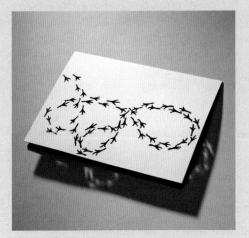

0131 : **CORAL & TUSK** : USA

0132 : **CORAL & TUSK** : USA

0133 : **CORAL & TUSK** : USA

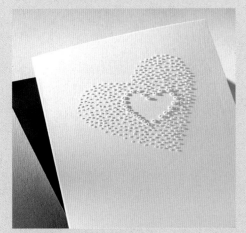

0134 : **WARPEDESIGN** : USA

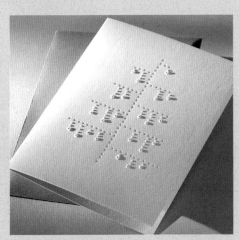

0135 : **WARPEDESIGN** : USA

0136 : **CORAL & TUSK** : USA

0137 : **CURIOUS GRAVY** : USA

0138 : **ART SCHOOL GIRL** : USA

0139 : **ART SCHOOL GIRL** : USA

0140 : **ART SCHOOL GIRL** : USA

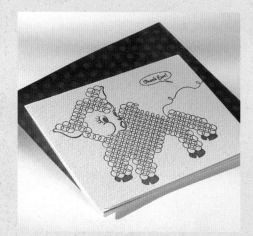

0142 : **PUP & PONY PRESS** : USA

0143 : **PUP & PONY PRESS** : USA

0144 : **PUP & PONY PRESS** : USA

0145 : **WE ARE MESSENGERS** : AUSTRALIA

0146 : **WE ARE MESSENGERS** : AUSTRALIA

0147 : **WE ARE MESSENGERS** : AUSTRALIA

0148 : **WE ARE MESSENGERS** : AUSTRALIA

0149 : **PUP & PONY PRESS** : USA

0150 : **PUP & PONY PRESS** : USA

0151 : **PRODUCT SUPERIOR** : USA

0152 : **PRODUCT SUPERIOR** : USA

0153 : **PRODUCT SUPERIOR** : USA

0154 : **PRODUCT SUPERIOR** : USA

0155 : **PRODUCT SUPERIOR** : USA

0156 : **PRODUCT SUPERIOR** : USA

0157 : **PRODUCT SUPERIOR** : USA

0158 : **PRODUCT SUPERIOR** : USA

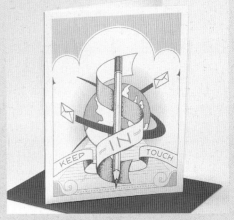

0159 : **PRODUCT SUPERIOR** : USA

0161 : **THE HIVE DESIGN STUDIO** : USA

0162 : **THE HIVE DESIGN STUDIO** : USA

0163 : **THE HIVE DESIGN STUDIO** : USA

0164 : **THE HIVE DESIGN STUDIO** : USA

0166 : **THE HIVE DESIGN STUDIO** : USA

0165 : **THE HIVE DESIGN STUDIO** : USA

0167 : **ANAGRAM PRESS & IGLOO LETTERPRESS** : USA

0168 : **HEARTS & ANCHORS** : USA

0169 : **ANAGRAM PRESS & IGLOO LETTERPRESS** : USA

0170 : **HEARTS & ANCHORS** : USA

0172 : **ORANGEBEAUTIFUL** : USA

0173 : **ORANGEBEAUTIFUL** : USA

0174 : **ORANGEBEAUTIFUL** : USA

0175 : **ORANGEBEAUTIFUL** : USA

0178 : **LEAD GRAFFITI** : USA

0179 : **LEAD GRAFFITI** : USA

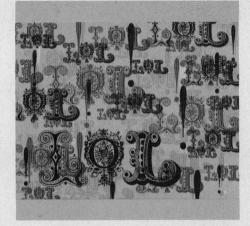

0180 : **LEAD GRAFFITI** : USA

0181 : **SYCAMORE STREET PRESS** : USA

0182 : **LEAD GRAFFITI** : USA

0183 : **LEAD GRAFFITI** : USA

0184 : **LEAD GRAFFITI** : USA

0185 : **LEAD GRAFFITI** : USA

0186 : **LEAD GRAFFITI** : USA

0187 : **LEAD GRAFFITI** : USA

0188 : **LEAD GRAFFITI** : USA

0189 : **LEAD GRAFFITI** : USA

0190 : **LEAD GRAFFITI** : USA

For the latke lover in you.

0191 : **SELTZER, LLC** : USA

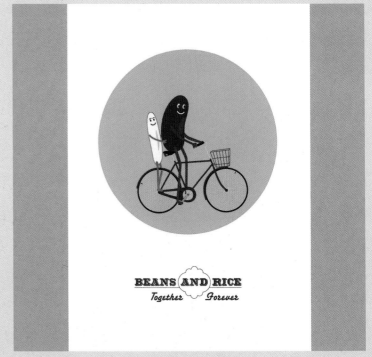

"You shouldn't have!"
Beans & Rice

0192 : **SELTZER, LLC** : USA

Time to break out your best moves.

0193 : **SELTZER, LLC** : USA

BEANS AND RICE
Together Forever

0194 : **SELTZER, LLC** : USA

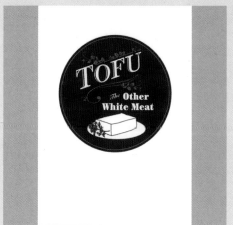

0195 : **SELTZER, LLC** : USA

0196 : **POP + SHORTY** : USA

0197 : **CRACKED DESIGNS LLC** : USA

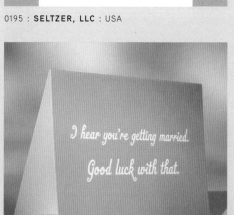

0198 : **POP + SHORTY** : USA

0199 : **DUDE AND CHICK** : USA

0200 : **ANDY PRATT DESIGN** : USA

0201 : **ANDY PRATT DESIGN** : USA

0202 : **THE HIVE DESIGN STUDIO** : USA

0203 : **POP + SHORTY** : USA

0205 : **THE PAPER NUT** : USA

0206 : **THE PAPER NUT** : USA

0207 : **THE PAPER NUT** : USA

0208 : **THE PAPER NUT** : USA

0209 : **PAPER RELICS** : USA

0210 : **PAPER RELICS** : USA

0211 : **PAPER RELICS** : USA

0212 : **LEAD GRAFFITI** : USA

0213 : **LEAD GRAFFITI** : USA

0214 : **LEAD GRAFFITI** : USA

0215 : **SYCAMORE STREET PRESS** : USA

0216 : **PAPER RELICS** : USA

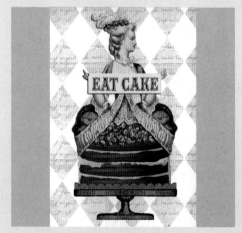

0217 : **PAPER RELICS** : USA

You're a good egg

0219 : **DUDE AND CHICK** : USA

0220 : **BANDITO DESIGN CO.** : USA

0221 : **PANCAKE & FRANKS** : USA

0222 : **CUTIEPIE COMPANY** : USA

0223 : **GREENWICH LETTERPRESS** : USA

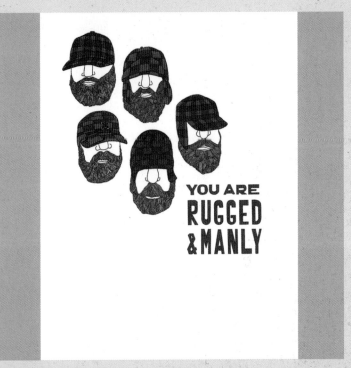

0224 : **DUDE AND CHICK** : USA

0225 : **DUDE AND CHICK** : USA

0226 : **PANCAKE & FRANKS** : USA

0227 : **MOOMAH** : USA

0228 : **MOOMAH** : USA

0229 : **MOOMAH** : USA

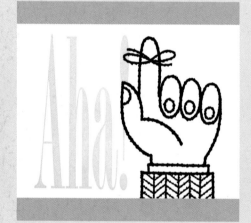

0230 : **LEAD GRAFFITI** : USA

0231 : **LEAD GRAFFITI** : USA

0232 : **LEAD GRAFFITI** : USA

0233 : **EMILY ANN DESIGNS** : USA

0234 : **EMILY ANN DESIGNS** : USA

0235 : **EMILY ANN DESIGNS** : USA

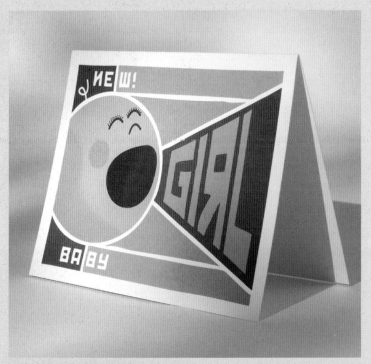

0240 : **ANDY PRATT DESIGN** : USA

0241 : **ANDY PRATT DESIGN** : USA

0242 : **POP + SHORTY** : USA

0243 : **ANDY PRATT DESIGN** : USA

0245 : **RIFLE PAPER CO** : USA

0246 : **RIFLE PAPER CO** : USA

0247 : **RIFLE PAPER CO** : USA

0248 : **RIFLE PAPER CO** : USA

0249 : **RIFLE PAPER CO** : USA

0250 : **RIFLE PAPER CO** : USA

A flock of hateful pigeons

My head hurts

With such a tiny brain, it can't hurt that much

And your ass is fat

I don't think you belong in this square, dear

Get stuffed

Just hearing your voice gives ME a headache

Is that pink natural?

It's because you eat so much garbage

0252 : **WHIGBY** : CANADA

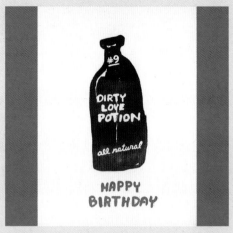

0251 : **WHIGBY** : CANADA

fill in the state & check a box!

☐ WISH YOU WERE HERE!
☐ I WISH I WAS VISITING YOU IN...
☐ THANKS FOR THE VISIT!
☐ GREETINGS FROM...

0253 : **THE PERMANENT COLLECTION** : USA

You Complete Me

0254 : **WHIGBY** : CANADA

0255 : **WHIGBY** : CANADA

0256 : **WHIGBY** : CANADA

Peace

0257 : **WHIGBY** : CANADA

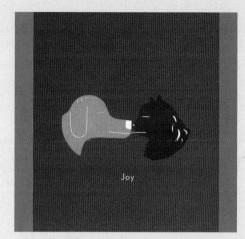

Joy

0258 : **WHIGBY** : CANADA

Love

0259 : **WHIGBY** : CANADA

FALLING

0260 : **WHIGBY** : CANADA

head

heels

0261 : **WHIGBY** : CANADA

I WILL LOVE YOU
UNTIL THE DAY I DIE
(UNLESS YOU DIE FIRST)

0262 : **WHIGBY** : CANADA

0263 : **WHIGBY** : CANADA

0264 : **WHIGBY** : CANADA

0265 : **WHIGBY** : CANADA

0266 : **WHIGBY** : CANADA

I went into a store looking for a card to give to you. When I saw this one, I said to myself (quietly because there were other people milling about), "This is it, this is the perfect card for...you!" There were lots of cards in that store. Many rows with tall card racks filled to capacity. True, some of the cards were located on shelves that were rather low and I couldn't be bothered bending down to see them. Nevertheless, none spoke to me in quite the same way that this one did. Was it the flawless flatness of the thing? Perhaps the crease centered so perfectly along the spine? I was transfixed and I couldn't imagine not buying this card for you. So I took it to the counter and paid for it. It was a bit expensive, but well worth it. When I arrived home, I slipped the card into the matching envelope and wrote your name on it. But enough about me. Happy Birthday.

0267 : **WHIGBY** : CANADA

I was trying to find the perfect words. I spent months combing through the *Oxford English Dictionary* (not the *Compact* or *Concise* versions). I studied books of quotations (in all the Romantic languages) and thesauri galore. I Googled and I doodled. I asked friends and acquaintances (some in high places) if they knew. Several scoffed and said, "There are no words, you idiot." Others simply said, "Go away, I'm busy." One close friend confessed that she'd spent the better part of her life looking for the words and never had any luck. Unabated, I continued searching. Years passed. Decades! Then one day I wandered absentmindedly (for by this time I was very old) into a shop and picked up a boring blue greeting card that I found on a shelf. When I came to the final two words, I knew I had found what I was looking for. "Happy Birthday," it said. Happy Birthday.

0268 : **WHIGBY** : CANADA

Sad You Went Away

0269 : **JAMIE LATENDRESSE DESIGN** : USA

Nice Seeing **You.**

0270 : **JAMIE LATENDRESSE DESIGN** : USA

0271 : **TAD CARPENTER**/**VAHALLA** : USA

0272 : **TAD CARPENTER**/**VAHALLA** : USA

0273 : **TAD CARPENTER**/**VAHALLA** : USA

0274 : **TAD CARPENTER**/**VAHALLA** : USA

0275 : **TAD CARPENTER**/**VAHALLA** : USA

0280 : **CROWDED TEETH** : USA

0281 : **CROWDED TEETH** : USA

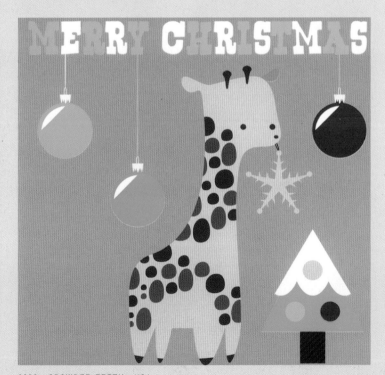

0282 : **CROWDED TEETH** : USA

0283 : **CROWDED TEETH** : USA

HAPPY ANNIVERSARY

0284 : **CROWDED TEETH** : USA

0285 : **CROWDED TEETH** : USA

HATS OFF TO YOU!

0286 : **CROWDED TEETH** : USA

MUCH LOVE

0287 : **CROWDED TEETH** : USA

NEW HOME

0288 : **CROWDED TEETH** : USA

HEY BABY

0289 : **CROWDED TEETH** : USA

0290 : **CROWDED TEETH** : USA

0291 : **CROWDED TEETH** : USA

0292 : **CROWDED TEETH** : USA

0293 : **CROWDED TEETH** : USA

0294 : **CROWDED TEETH** : USA

0295 : **CROWDED TEETH** : USA

0296 : **CROWDED TEETH** : USA

0297 : **CROWDED TEETH** : USA

0298 : **CROWDED TEETH** : USA

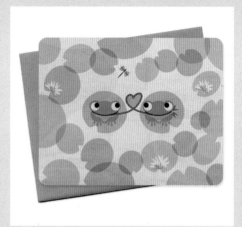

0299 : **NIGHT OWL PAPER GOODS** : USA

i love you a
whole latté

0300 : **NIGHT OWL PAPER GOODS** : USA

0301 : **NIGHT OWL PAPER GOODS** : USA

: buck up, buttercup! :

0302 : **NIGHT OWL PAPER GOODS** : USA

0303 : **NIGHT OWL PAPER GOODS** : USA

I LOVE YOU

0304 : **NIGHT OWL PAPER GOODS** : USA

0305 : **NIGHT OWL PAPER GOODS** : USA

0306 : **NIGHT OWL PAPER GOODS** : USA

0307 : **NIGHT OWL PAPER GOODS** : USA

0308 : **NIGHT OWL PAPER GOODS** : USA

0309 : **YEE-HAW INDUSTRIES** : USA

0310 : **YEE-HAW INDUSTRIES** : USA

0311 : **YEE-HAW INDUSTRIES** : USA

0312 : **YEE-HAW INDUSTRIES** : USA

0313 : **YEE-HAW INDUSTRIES** : USA

0314 : **YEE-HAW INDUSTRIES** : USA

0315 : **YEE-HAW INDUSTRIES** : USA

0316 : **YEE-HAW INDUSTRIES** : USA

0317 : **TAD CARPENTER**/VAHALLA : USA

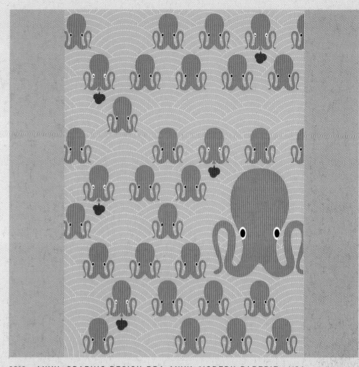

0318 : ANVIL GRAPHIC DESIGN DBA ANVIL MODERN PAPERIE : USA

0319 : ANVIL GRAPHIC DESIGN DBA ANVIL MODERN PAPERIE : USA

0320 : ANVIL GRAPHIC DESIGN DBA ANVIL MODERN PAPERIE : USA

0321 : ANVIL GRAPHIC DESIGN DBA ANVIL MODERN PAPERIE : USA

0322 : **TAD CARPENTER**/**VAHALLA** : USA

0323 : **TAD CARPENTER**/**VAHALLA** : USA

0324 : **TAD CARPENTER**/**VAHALLA** : USA

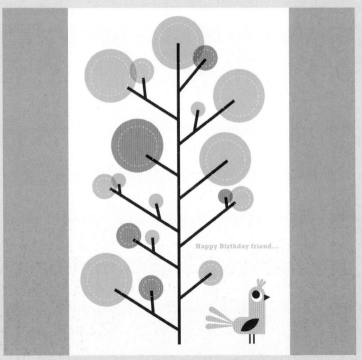

0325 : **TAD CARPENTER**/**VAHALLA** : USA

0327 : **TAD CARPENTER**/**VAHALLA** : USA

0328 : **TAD CARPENTER**/**VAHALLA** : USA

THE BEST
SHENANIGANS...

0329 : **TAD CARPENTER**/**VAHALLA** : USA

0330 : **TAD CARPENTER**/**VAHALLA** : USA

0331 : **WHIGBY** : CANADA

0332 : **WHIGBY** : CANADA

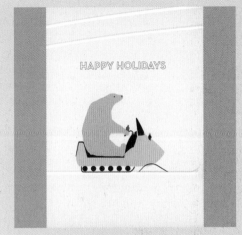

0333 : **WHIGBY** : CANADA

0334 : **TAD** CARPENTER / **VAHALLA** : USA

0335 : **TAD** CARPENTER / **VAHALLA** : USA

0336 : **TAD** CARPENTER / **VAHALLA** : USA

0337 : **TAD** CARPENTER / **VAHALLA** : USA

0338 : **TAD** CARPENTER / **VAHALLA** : USA

0339 : **ORANGEBEAUTIFUL** : USA

0340 : **ORANGEBEAUTIFUL** : USA

0341 : **ORANGEBEAUTIFUL** : USA

0342 : **ORANGEBEAUTIFUL** : USA

0343 : **HIJIRIK STUDIO** : USA

0344 : **HIJIRIK STUDIO** : USA

0345 : **HIJIRIK STUDIO** : USA

0346 : **HIJIRIK STUDIO** : USA

0347 : **THE CARTE POSTALE** : UK

0348 : **THE CARTE POSTALE** : UK

0349 : **THE CARTE POSTALE** : UK

0350 : **THE CARTE POSTALE** : UK

0351 : **THE CARTE POSTALE** : UK

0352 : **THE CARTE POSTALE** : UK

0353 : **THE CARTE POSTALE** : UK

0354 : **EMILY ANN DESIGNS** : USA

0356 : **GREENWICH LETTERPRESS** : USA

0357 : **GILAH PRESS + DESIGN** : USA

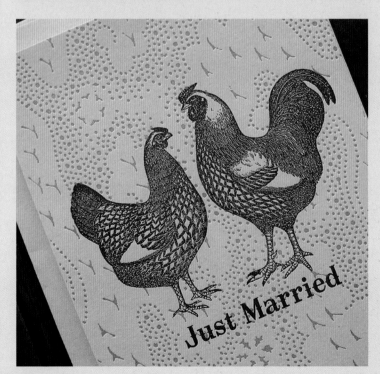

0358 : **GREENWICH LETTERPRESS** : USA

0359 : **DESIGN DES TROY** : USA

0360 : **RIFLE PAPER CO.** : USA

0361 : **PAPER SCHMAPER** : USA

0362 : **PAPER SCHMAPER** : USA

0363 : **RIFLE PAPER CO.** : USA

0364 : **RIFLE PAPER CO.** : USA

0365 : **KIRTLAND HOUSE PRESS** : USA

0366–0373 : **KAMAL** : USA

0374 : **ANAGRAM PRESS & IGLOO LETTERPRESS** : USA

0376 : **KIRTLAND HOUSE PRESS** : USA

0377 : **PAPER SCHMAPER** : USA

0378 : **KIRTLAND HOUSE PRESS** : USA

0379 : **KIRTLAND HOUSE PRESS** : USA

0380 : **PAPER SCHMAPER** : USA

0381 : **RUBY VICTORIA LETTERPRESS + PRINTMAKING** : AUSTRALIA

0382 : **HULDRA PRESS** : USA

0383 : **HULDRA PRESS** : USA

0384 : **GILAH PRESS + DESIGN** : USA

0385 : **WONDER WONDER** : USA

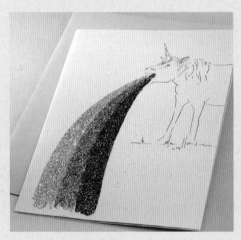

0386 : **CASSIE HESTER DESIGN + ILLUSTRATION** : USA

0387 : **ORANGEBEAUTIFUL** : USA

0388 : **PLAZM** : USA

0389 : **HULDRA PRESS** : USA

DING DONG!
RING A LING LING!
THUMPETTY!
THUMP THUMP!
FA LA LA LA LAAA!
LA LA LA LA!
WHOOP DE DO!
JINGLE JINGLE
HO! HO! HOOOO!
PAAAAA RUM
PUM PUM PUM!
RUM PUM PUM PUM!
RUM PUM PUM
PUMMMMMM!
HALLELUJAH!

0390 : **AYA IKEGAYA** : USA

0391 : **THE PERMANENT COLLECTION** : USA

HELLO

0392 : **HULDRA PRESS** : USA

0393 : **HULDRA PRESS** : USA

HAPPY holidays & SEASONS Greetings

0394 : **HULDRA PRESS** : USA

ho ho ho

0395 : **HULDRA PRESS** : USA

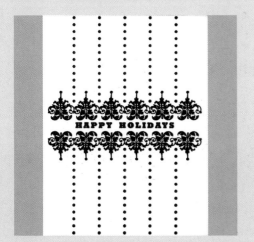

HAPPY HOLIDAYS

0396 : **THE PERMANENT COLLECTION** : USA

JOY ♂ U this christmas!

0397 : **THE PERMANENT COLLECTION** : USA

0398 : **OBLATION PAPERS + PRESS** : USA

0399 : **OBLATION PAPERS + PRESS** : USA

0400 : **GILAH PRESS + DESIGN** : USA

0402 : **BANDITO DESIGN CO.** : USA

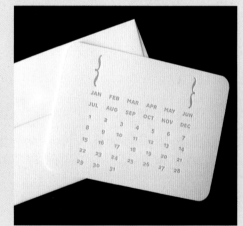

0401 : **HIJIRIK STUDIO** : USA

0403 : **HIJIRIK STUDIO** : USA

Dear _____,

Occasion (place check mark next to occasion of choice):

☐ Birthday   ☐ New Job
☐ Graduation   ☐ Lost Your Job
☐ Wedding   ☐ Under the Weather
☐ Anniversary   ☐ Brand New Pet
☐ New Baby   ☐ Thinking of You
☐ Housewarming   ☐ Forgot about You

Sentiment (place check mark next to chosen sentiment):

☐ Enjoy your day!   ☐ I'm so lonely.
☐ Congratulations!   ☐ I'm sorry to hear it.
☐ You're so pretty.   ☐ So happy to hear it
☐ You're so handsome.   ☐ You don't look well.
☐ You look so thin!   ☐ I don't look well.
☐ Are you heavier?   ☐ Where are my keys?
☐ Hug that baby!   ☐ You're in jail?
☐ Change that baby!   ☐ Why am I in jail?
☐ What's its name?   ☐ I like your hair.
☐ What's my name?   ☐ I hate your hair.
☐ What's your name?   ☐ I miss you.

Love, _____

PreMade Correspondence by JamieBert   ©2009 JamieBert. All Rights Reserved.

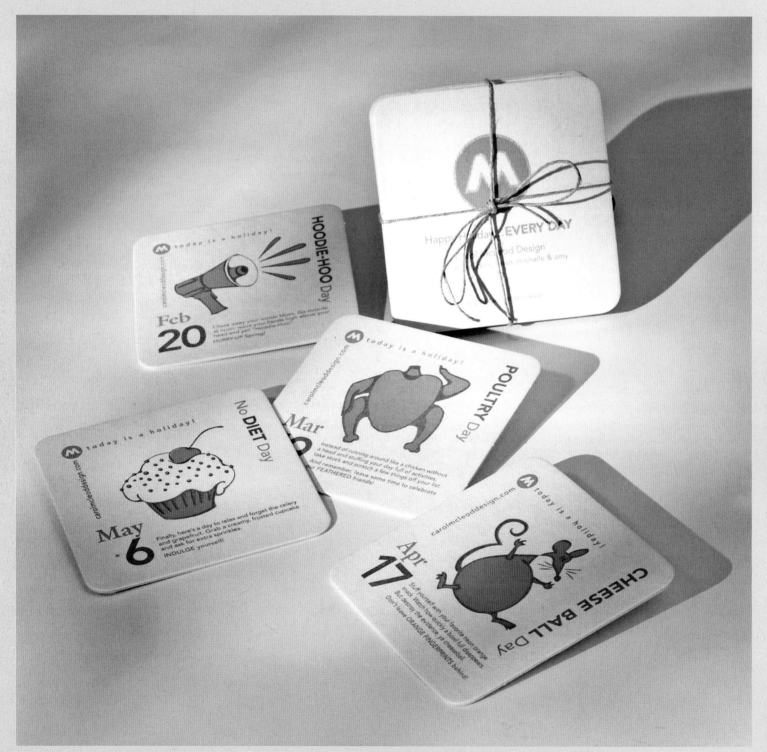

0406 : **CHRIS ROONEY ILLUSTRATION/DESIGN** : USA

0407 : **DESIGN DES TROY** : USA

0408 : ❯**PROMPTT** : USA

0409 : ❯**PROMPTT** : USA

0413 : **GIANESINI DESIGN** : USA

0414 : **ACME INDUSTRIES** : ROMANIA

0415 : **TOPOS GRAPHICS** : USA

0416 : **OCTAVIUS MURRAY** : UK

I recommend
Vodka

0417 : **OBLATION PAPERS + PRESS** : USA

Children
will ruin your life

0418 : **OBLATION PAPERS + PRESS** : USA

Socialism
it's not just
for
Europeans
anymore

0419 : **OBLATION PAPERS + PRESS** : USA

0420 : **OBLATION PAPERS + PRESS** : USA

0421 : **OBLATION PAPERS + PRESS** : USA

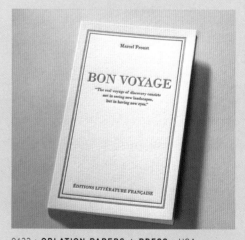

0422 : **OBLATION PAPERS + PRESS** : USA

0423 : **OBLATION PAPERS + PRESS** : USA

0424 : **OBLATION PAPERS + PRESS** : USA

0425 : **OBLATION PAPERS + PRESS** : USA

0427 : **SERAPH DESIGN** : USA

0428 : **GRETEMAN GROUP** : USA

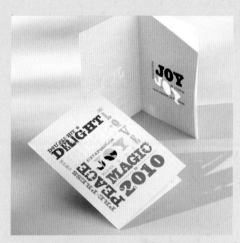

0429 : **WHITE RHINO** : USA

0430 : **ELEMENTS** : USA

0431 : **RULE 29** : USA

0432 : **MILES DESIGN** : USA

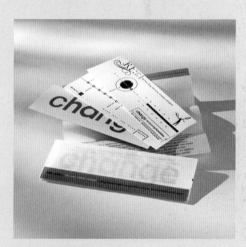

0433 : **HA DESIGN** : USA

0434 : **DAVID SENIOR** : USA

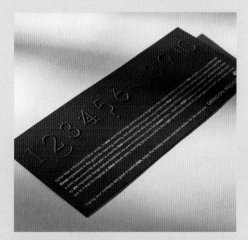

0435 : **DRAGON ROUGE** : USA

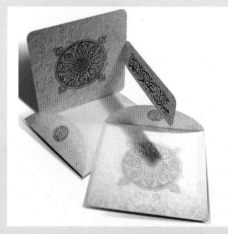

0436 : **PARAGON MARKETING COMMUNICATIONS** : KUWAIT

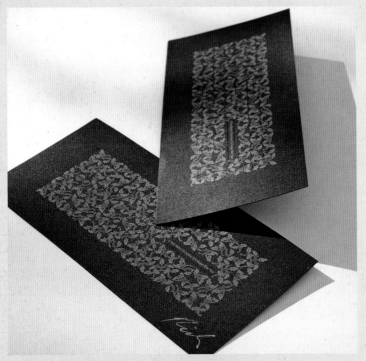

0437 : **P22 TYPE FOUNDRY** : USA

0438 : **TIMBER DESIGN CO.** : USA

0439 : **TIMBER DESIGN CO.** : USA

0440 : **TIMBER DESIGN CO.** : USA

0443 : **PARAGON MARKETING COMMUNICATIONS** : KUWAIT

0444 : **GRETEMAN GROUP** : USA

0445 : **GRETEMAN GROUP** : USA

0446 : **TOKY BRANDING + DESIGN** : USA

0447 : **GEYRHALTER DESIGN** : USA

0448 : **MANUEL OLMO/OLMOCS** : USA

0449 : **GILAH PRESS + DESIGN** : USA

0450 : **FINISHED ART INC.** : USA

0451 : **ZINNOBERGRUEN GMBH** : GERMANY

0452 : **MILCH DESIGN GMBH** : GERMANY

0453 : **MENAGERIE CREATIVE** : USA

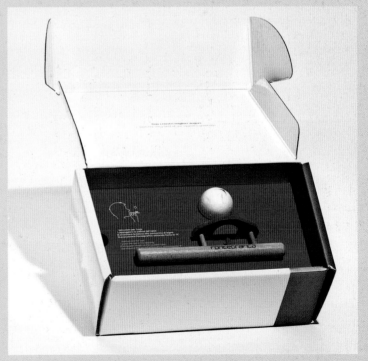

0454 : **CACAO DESIGN** : ITALY

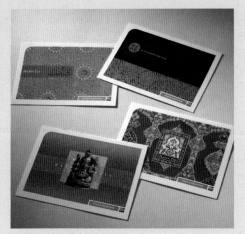

0456 : **WING CHAN DESIGN, INC.** : USA

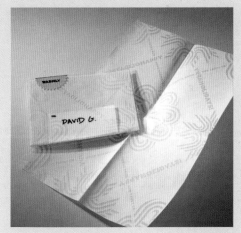

0457 : **TOPOS GRAPHICS** : USA

0458 : **GROSSET & DUNLAP (AN IMPRINT OF PENGUIN PUBLISHERS)** : USA

0459 : **CUTIEPIE COMPANY** : USA

0460 : **WE ARE MESSENGERS** : AUSTRALIA

0461 : **WING CHAN DESIGN, INC.** : USA

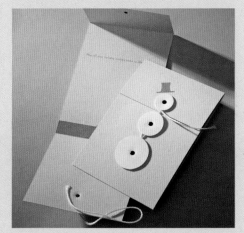

0462 : **DAVID CLARK DESIGN** : USA

0463 : **PYLON** : CANADA

0464 : **GAGATREE PTE LTD** : SINGAPORE

0465 : **PILLAR IN-HOUSE CREATIVE** : USA

0466 : **EMILIA LÓPEZ** : AUSTRIA

0467 : **TOPOS GRAPHICS** : USA

0468 : **R DESIGN** : UK

0470 : **RUTH HUIMERIND** : ESTONIA

0471 : **ZYNC** : CANADA

0472 : **MICHAEL OSBORNE DESIGN AND JOEY'S CORNER** : USA

0473 : **THOMAS MANSS & CO** : UK

hatch

Greetings From Your Friends at Hatch,

We hope you've had a great year! Here at Hatch, things have been hopping...creating work for our great clients, and "hatching" our very own wine company (be sure to check out jaqkcellars.com).

And now, we're here to help you get in the spirit of the season with our exclusive Jumping JAQK toy. Easy to assemble, it's guaranteed to lift your holiday spirits!

of luck in the New Year,

, Joel, Eszter, Ryan, Shadi and Julie

reet
94133   T 415 398 1650
                 F 415 398 1660

                                    W hatchsf.com

0476 : **AYA IKEGAYA** : USA

0477 : **GOODESIGN** : USA

0478 : **GOODESIGN** : USA

0479 : **DONNA KARAN IN-HOUSE** : USA

0480 : **WORKTODATE** : USA

0481 : **PYLON** : CANADA

0482 : **ARAGON MARKETING COMMUNICATIONS** : KUWAIT

0483 : **REDBEAN DESIGN** : USA

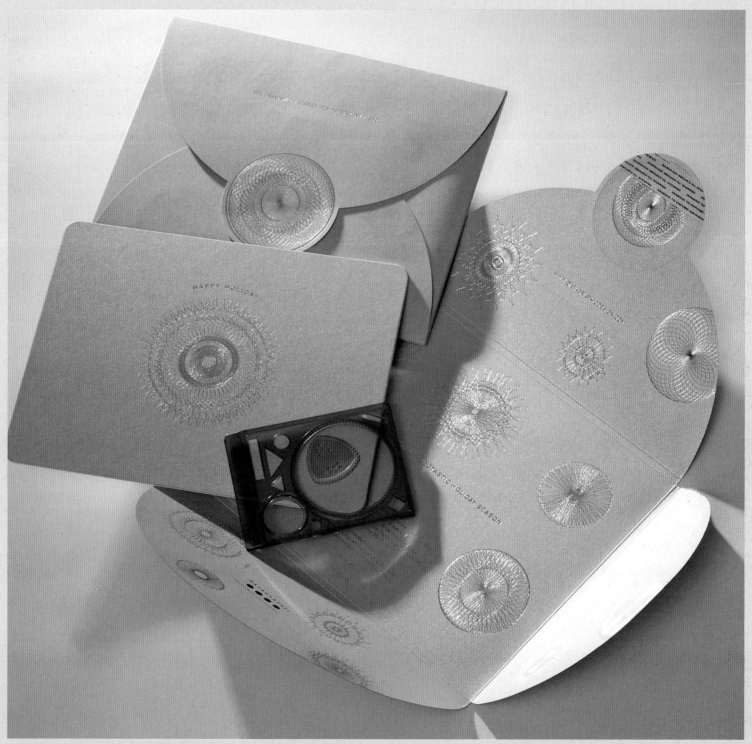

0486 : **GAGATREE PTE LTD** : SINGAPORE

0487 : **GAGATREE PTE LTD** : SINGAPORE

0488 : **GAGATREE PTE LTD** : SINGAPORE

0489 : **R DESIGN** : UK

Happy 2009 from Davies Associates

0490 : **DAVIES ASSOCIATES** : USA

MIX EQUAL PARTS ORANGE JUICE AND CRANBERRY JUICE, ADD TONIC WATER TO TASTE, STIR WELL AND GARNISH WITH A WEDGE OF LIME

DRAGON ROUGE
BRAND & DESIGN CONSULTING

MerryRedDragon

DRAGON ROUGE
BRAND & DESIGN CONSULTING

RED NECK ZOMBIE

3 oz lemon rum
1 oz blue curacao liqueur
4 oz citrus soda

combine and mix with ice
in a highball glass

DRAGON ROUGE
BRAND & DESIGN CONSULTING

1/2 oz lime juice, orange juice
1/2 oz vodka, 1/2 oz peach bourbon liqueur, 1/2 oz amaretto liqueur, 1/2 oz triple sec, 1/2 oz sloe gin, 1/2 oz
(except orange juice) into an ice-filled collins glass, add orange juice to taste
pour all ingredients

RED DEATH

DRAGON ROUGE
BRAND & DESIGN CONSULTING

RED FROG

1 oz raspberry liqueur
1 oz amaretto almond liqueur
1 oz whisky
2 oz cranberry juice
shake with ice and strain
into a highball glass with ice

THANKS FOR 2009, DRINK TO 2010.
DAVID & JEFF

SELECTISM.COM
TITELMEDIA.COM

HIGHSNOBIETY.COM
TITELMEDIA.COM

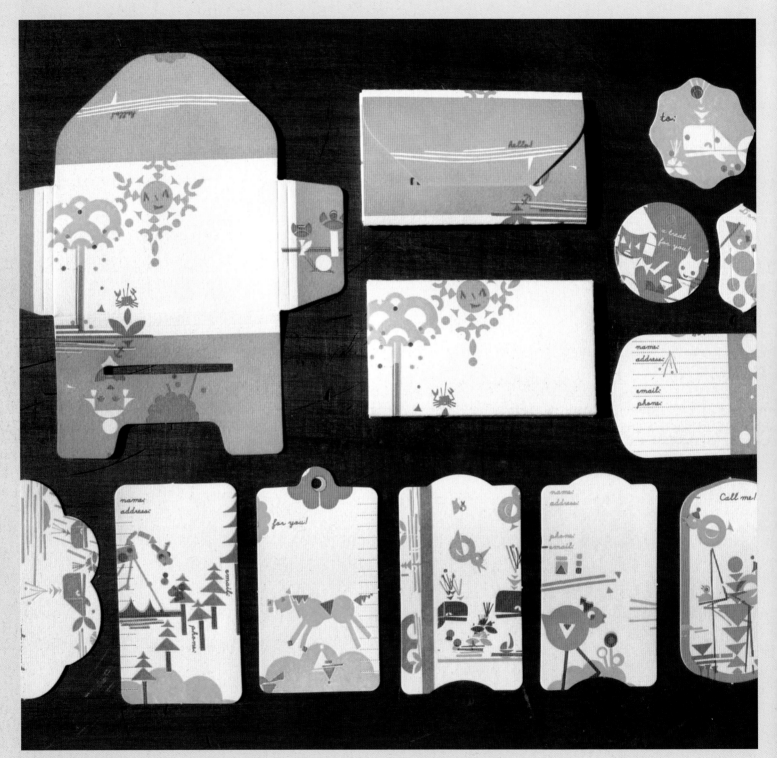

0494 : **ALAN VALEK** • **ART DIRECTION + GRAPHIC DESIGN** : USA

0495 : **STUDIO ON FIRE** : USA

0496 : **STUDIO ON FIRE** : USA

0497 : **STUDIO ON FIRE** : USA

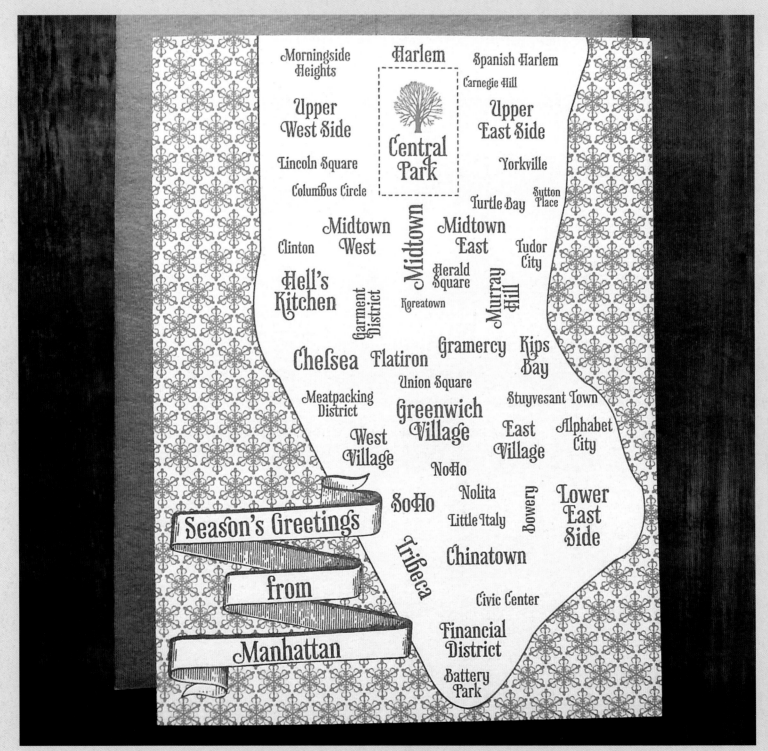

0499 : **CLEAR MARKETING** : UK

0500 : **MY ASSOCIATE CORNELIUS** : USA

0501 : **ELEVATED PRESS** : USA

0502 : **CHRIS ROONEY ILLUSTRATION/DESIGN** : USA

Leap at the chance to relax, reflect & rejuvenate. moag bailie

0503 : **MOAG BAILIE** : SOUTH AFRICA

0504 : **ZYNC** : CANADA

0505 : **SIMON & GOETZ DESIGN GMBH & CO. KG** : GERMANY

0506 : **ALEX PARROTT** : UK

0507 : **CRANKY PRESSMAN** : USA

0509 : **ART SCHOOL GIRL** : USA

0510 : **SHELBY DESIGNS & ILLUSTRATES** : USA

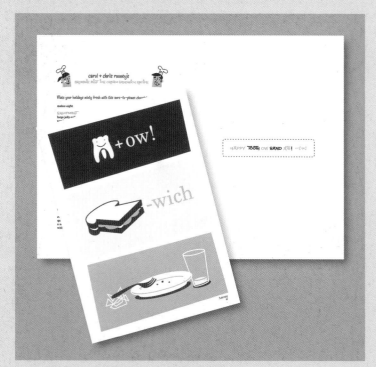

0511 : **CHRIS ROONEY ILLUSTRATION/DESIGN** : USA

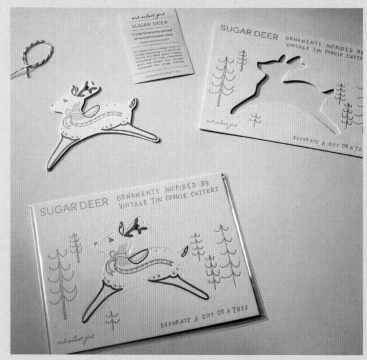

0512 : **ART SCHOOL GIRL** : USA

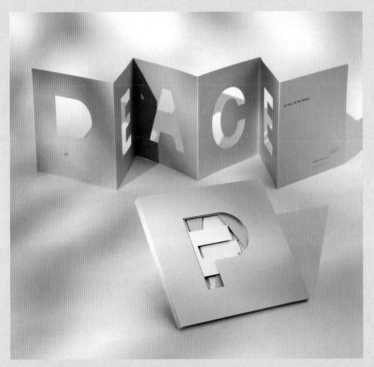

0513 : **DAVID CLARK DESIGN** : USA

0514 : **B.L.A. DESIGN COMPANY** : USA

0515 : **A3 DESIGN** : USA

0516 : **B.L.A. DESIGN COMPANY** : USA

DON'T LET THE REINDEER NEAR THE TREE.

A HOLIDAY TIP FROM ATOMICDUST

0517 : **ATOMIC DUST** : USA

DESPITE WHAT THE SONG SAYS, BIRDS MAKE A HORRIBLE GIFT.

A HOLIDAY TIP FROM ATOMICDUST

0518 : **ATOMIC DUST** : USA

DON'T DIE SHOVELING THE SNOW.

A HOLIDAY TIP FROM ATOMICDUST

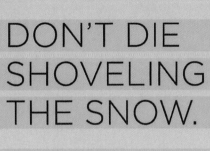

0519 : **ATOMIC DUST** : USA

GIVE A DIFFERENT TYPE OF NUTCRACKER THIS YEAR.

A HOLIDAY TIP FROM ATOMICDUST

0520 : **ATOMIC DUST** : USA

365 THINGS TO DO IN 2007

1. SPEND MORE TIME WITH THE KITTIES
2. SING IN THE SHOWER
3. DRINK MORE TEA
4. DRINK MORE TEQUILA
5. TAKE THE STAIRS
6. DO MY OWN LAUNDRY
7. FORGIVE AN ENEMY
8. LEARN TO PLAY AN INSTRUMENT
9. READ MY AT LEAST A MONTH
10. LEARN SPANISH
11. STAND UP STRAIGHT

12. MAKE A NEW FRIEND EVERY MONTH
13. CALL AN OLD FRIEND EVERY MONTH
14. DONATE THE CLOTHES I DIDN'T WEAR LAST YEAR
15. WEAR THE CLOTHES I DIDN'T DONATE LAST YEAR
16. BRING MY SEXY BACK

24. GO TO THE BRONX ZOO
26. JOIN A PARADE
27. MEET THE NEIGHBOR
28. GET A MOHAWK
30. MASTER THE ART OF READING LIPS

37. LEARN ITALIAN
38. QUIT DRINKING MILK
39. SKI THE SWISS ALPS
40. TRY OUT FOR AMERICAS NEXT TOP MODEL
41. VOLUNTEER AT A SOUP KITCHEN
42. START ANOTHER MASTER'S DEGREE
43. INVENT A NEW FORM OF YOGA
47. EAT FLAX SEEDS
48. DRIVE THE SPEED LIMIT
49. CALL MOM MORE OFTEN

50. STOP MAKING EXCUSES
51. VISIT THE LOWER EAST SIDE TENEMENT MUSEUM
52. SEND SOMEONE A CARD
53. BUY SOMETHING FROM WWW.JOINRED.COM AND SUPPORT THE FIGHT AGAINST AIDS IN AFRICA
54. DUST OFF THE HULA HOOP (IT'S BACK!!)
55. LEARN WHEN TO HOLD EM AND WHEN TO FOLD EM

56. EAT COPIOUS AMOUNTS OF CHOCOLATE
57. RENT OLD MOVIES
58. WALK TO WORK
59. ADOPT A PET (OR A CHILD)

62. SKIP WORK ON THE FIRST DAY OF FALL (AND WINTER, AND SUMMER, AND SPRING)
63. MAKE A SNOW ANGEL
64. VISIT CONEY ISLAND (RIDE THE CYCLONE)
65. TRASH MY TRASH
66. START CANNING 67. HAVE AN OFFICE PARTY 68. PLANT A TREE
69. STOP FEEDING THE SQUIRRELS HOMEMADE NUT CLUSTERS
70. USE EZ-PASS, PLEASZYPASS!
71. SELL MY OLD IPOD TO THE GUY IN UNION SQUARE
72. ORGANIZE MY RECIPES 73. SAVE A DOLLAR A DAY
74. LEARN TAI CHI

89. CLIMB THE STAIRS TO THE TOP OF THE EMPIRE STATE BUILDING
91. PLANT SOME BULBS
92. GO TO THE DENTIST
93. HOST MORE COCKTAIL PARTIES 94. FIND A BAR WITH $2.00 DRAFTS FOR HAPPY HOUR 95. GET A DRIVER'S LICENSE 96. BUY A HYBRID CAR
97. WALK ACROSS THE BROOKLYN BRIDGE AT LEAST ONCE A WEEK 98. ENROLL MY KID IN THEURBANNATURALISTS.COM
99. TAKE LUNCH BREAKS 100. WEAR MORE DRESSES 101. VISIT STOCKHOLM 102. BAKE BREAD
103. JOIN NETFLIX (FINALLY) 104. RENT THE ENTIRE FIRST AND SECOND SEASONS OF BATTLESTAR GALACTICA

105. BE ON TIME (LATENESS = LAMENESS)

106. LISTEN TO THE SONGBIRDS (THEY'RE SINGING FOR YOU)
107. EAT ORGANIC
108. START A BLOG
109. CREATE A NEW EXPERIENCE

122. BRING BACK THE PHRASE "AND HOW!"
123. REALLY TRY TO SEE IT FROM THEIR PERSPECTIVE 124. BUY PROPERTY IN NICARAGUA
125. REWATCH THE LAST SEASON OF THE WIRE (BECAUSE IT WAS SO DAMN GOOD!)
126. ATTEMPT TO DO VRSCHIKASANA (SCORPION POSE)

128. (AT LEAST ONCE) THROW MY HANDS IN THE AIR AND WAVE 'EM LIKE I JUST DON'T CARE

141. USE RECYCLED PAPER

Best of Luck.
GOODESIGN

HAPPY NEW YEAR!!

A SPECIAL DELIVERY FROM GOODESIGN: 55 JAY STREET, #901, BROOKLYN, NY 11201 | WWW.GOODESIGNNY.COM

0522 : **ANAGRAM PRESS & SPRINGTIDE PRESS** : USA

0523 : **ANAGRAM PRESS & SPRINGTIDE PRESS** : USA

0524 : **ANAGRAM PRESS & SPRINGTIDE PRESS** : USA

0525 : **INKY LIPS LETTERPRESS** : USA

0526 : **ANDY PRATT DESIGN** : USA

0527 : **AMBER JOSEY** : USA

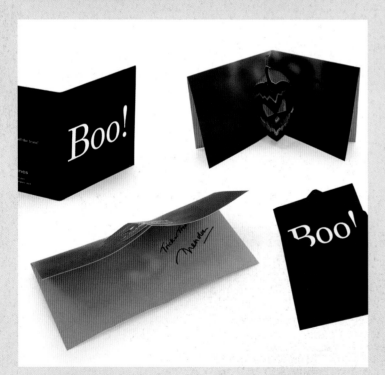

0528 : **DESIGNTACTICS** : IRELAND

0529 : **AERAKI** : GREECE

0531 : **HATCH DESIGN** : USA

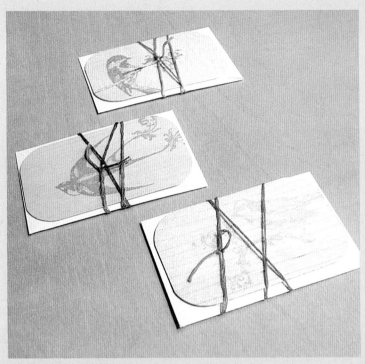

0532 : **CABIN + CUB DESIGN** : USA

0533 : **GILAH PRESS + DESIGN** : USA

0534 : **THE PAPER NUT** : USA

BON NADAL
FELIZ NAVIDAD
MERRY CHRISTMAS

SERIES NEMO
2009

Branding
Diseño de producto
Packaging
Web

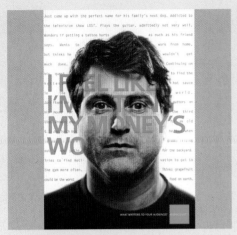

0537 : **ATOMIC DUST** : USA

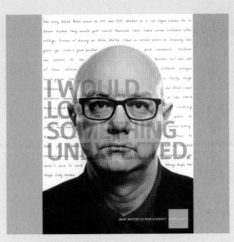

0538 : **ATOMIC DUST** : USA

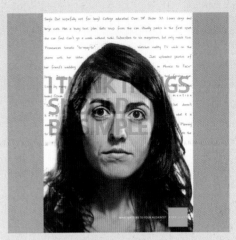

0539 : **ATOMIC DUST** : USA

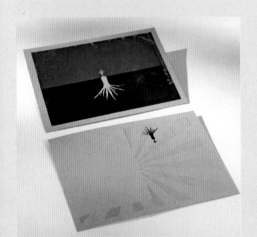

0540 : **EP DESIGNWORKS** : USA

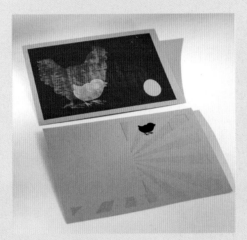

0541 : **EP DESIGNWORKS** : USA

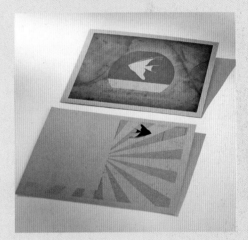

0542 : **EP DESIGNWORKS** : USA

0543 : **HONEST BROS** : USA

0544 : **HONEST BROS** : USA

0545 : **HONEST BROS** : USA

0546 : **CACAO DESIGN** : ITALY

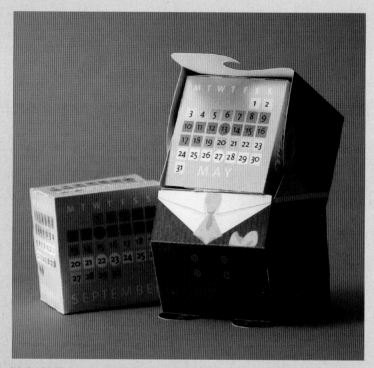

0547 : **BURO-LAMP** : AMSTERDAM, NETHERLANDS

0548 : **YOUNG & RUBICAM** : UNITED ARAB EMIRATES

0549 : **DAIS** : AUSTRALIA

0550 : **CHRIS TRIVIZAS I DESIGN** : GREECE

0551 : **CHRIS TRIVIZAS I DESIGN** : GREECE

0552 : **R DESIGN** : UK

0553 : **COPIA CREATIVE, INC.** : USA

The market is always good for new friends.

A good relationship appreciates in value.

A warm smile can greatly improve your "curb appeal."

KELLER WILLIAMS

0556 : **YOUNG & RUBICAM** : UNITED ARAB EMIRATES

0557 : **SELTZER, LLC** : USA

0558 : **R DESIGN** : USA

0559 : **BRONSON MA CREATIVE** : USA

0562 : **BARNHART** : USA

0563 : **COPIA CREATIVE, INC.** : USA

0564 : **BARNHART** : USA

0565 : **HATCH DESIGN** : USA

0566 : **COPIA CREATIVE, INC.** : USA

0567 : **NICOLE LAVELLE** : USA

0568 : **ROME & GOLD CREATIVE** : USA

0569 : **ANDY BABB** : USA

0570 : **MIRIELLO GRAFICO** : USA

0571 : **HALEY STUDIO** : USA

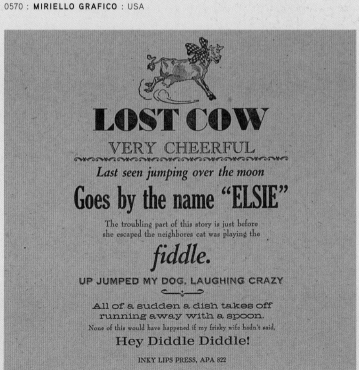

0572 : **INKY LIPS LETTERPRESS** : USA

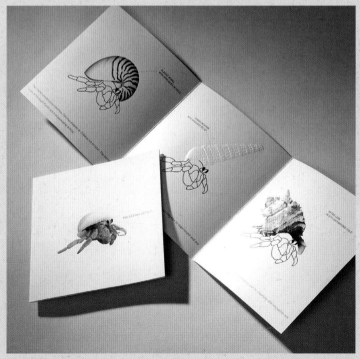

0573 : **ZINNOBERGRUEN GMBH** : GERMANY

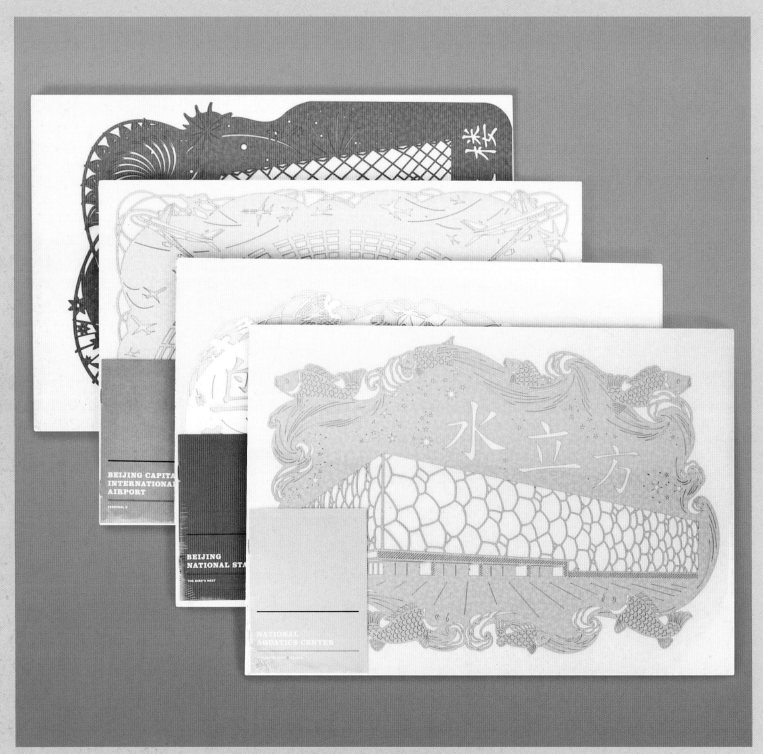

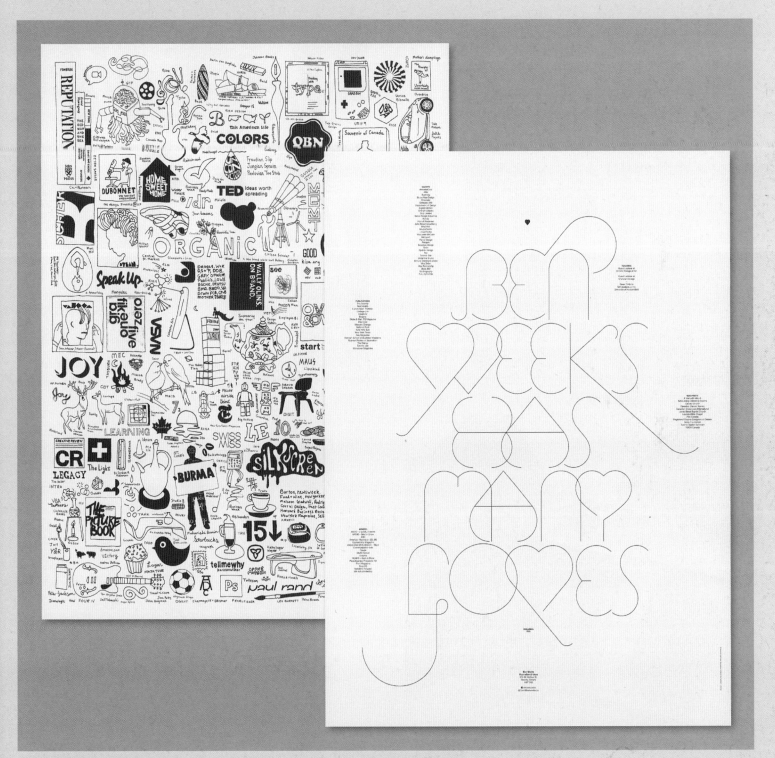

0576 : **BARNHART** : USA

0577 : **JONATHAN BARTLETT** : USA

0578 : **ELEVEN1111ELEVEN DESIGN** : AUSTRALIA

0579 : **GOODESIGN** : USA

SELFRIDGES&Cº
OWN BRAND PACKAGING DESIGN

by R Design, visit
www.r-website.co.uk

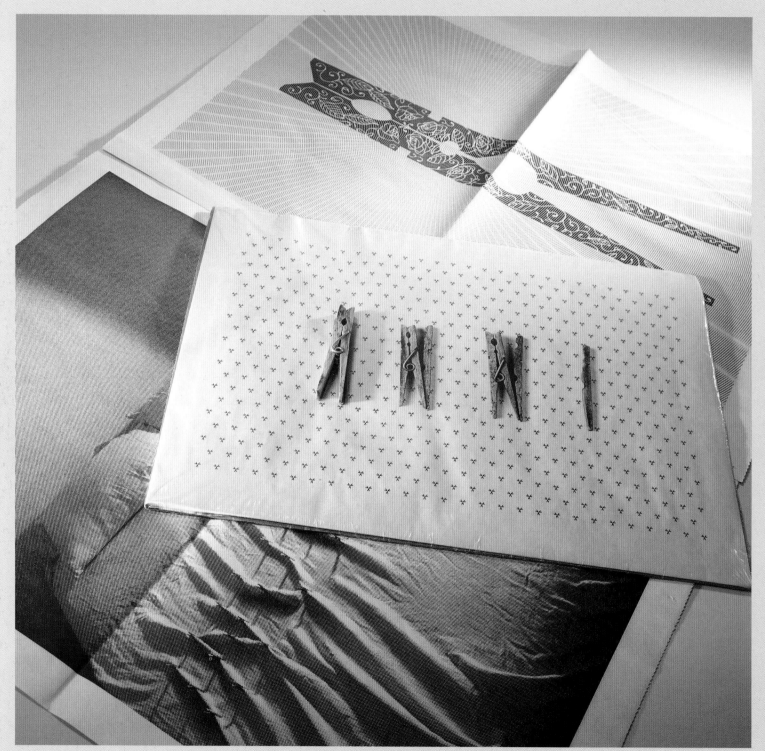

ANNI KUAN

HAPPILY INVITES YOU TO PREVIEW THE FALL AND WINTER 2008 COLLECTION AT THE
FASHION COTERIE FROM SUNDAY, FEBRUARY 10th TO TUESDAY, FEBRUARY 12th 2008,
THE JAVITS CENTER, NEW YORK CITY.

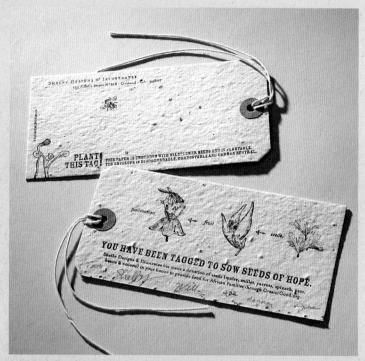

0583 : **SHELBY DESIGNS & ILLUSTRATES** : USA

0584 : **CRANKY PRESSMAN** : USA

0585 : **SUBSTANCE151** : USA

0586 : **CRANKY PRESSMAN** : USA

0587 : **COPIA CREATIVE, INC.** : USA

0588 : **LITTLE JACKET** : USA

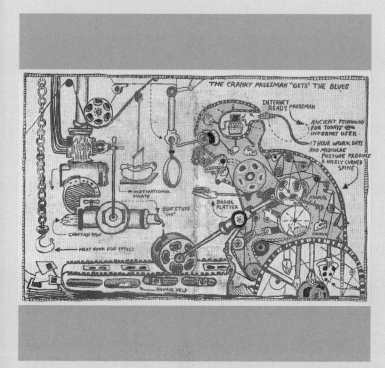

0589 : **LITTLE JACKET** : USA

0590 : **LITTLE JACKET** : USA

0592 : **HELIX** : USA

0593 : **MIRIELLO GRAFICO** : USA

0594 : **FOREIGN POLICY DESIGN GROUP** : SINGAPORE

0595 : **FOREIGN POLICY DESIGN GROUP** : SINGAPORE

0596 : **FOREIGN POLICY DESIGN GROUP** : SINGAPORE

0597 : **RULE 29** : USA

0598 : **ZEITHEIST PRODUCTIONS** : USA

0599 : **MR. FANCY PANTS** : USA

0600 : **RUBBER DESIGN** : USA

0601 : **GRAVES FOWLER CREATIVE** : USA

0602 : **ROUGHSTOCK STUDIOS** : USA

04 ANNOUNCEMENTS

0605 : **COOPER GRAPHIC DESIGN** : USA

0606 : **THE NBC AGENCY** : USA

0607 : **TIMBER DESIGN CO.** : USA

0608 : **GOODESIGN** : USA

0609 : **TOPOS GRAPHICS** : USA

0610 : **GOODESIGN** : USA

0611 : **JULIA REICH DESIGN** : USA

0612 : **BANDITO DESIGN CO.** : USA

0613 : **CASSIE HESTER DESIGN + ILLUSTRATION** : USA

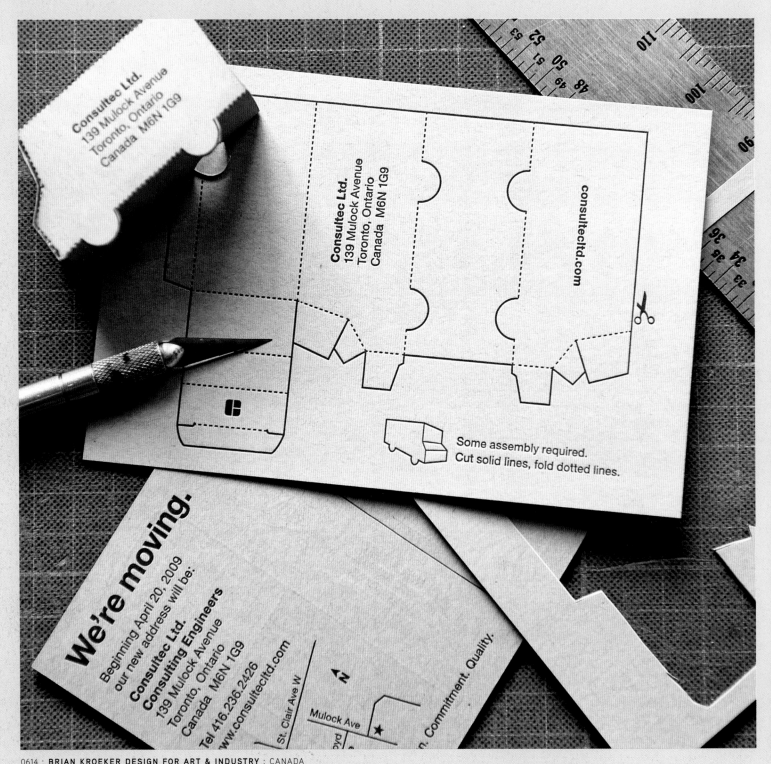

Consultec Ltd.
139 Mulock Avenue
Toronto, Ontario
Canada M6N 1G9

consultecltd.com

Some assembly required.
Cut solid lines, fold dotted lines.

We're moving.

Beginning April 20, 2009
our new address will be:

Consultec Ltd.
Consulting Engineers
139 Mulock Avenue
Toronto, Ontario
Canada M6N 1G9
Tel 416.236.2426
www.consultecltd.com

St. Clair Ave W
Mulock Ave

n. Commitment. Quality.

0615 : **PRODUCT SUPERIOR** : USA

0616 : **PENCIL** : UK

0617 : **OBLATION PAPERS + PRESS** : USA

0618 : **LYNNE DOOR** : USA

IT'S A GIRL!

BORN MARCH 5, 2009 AT 2:03AM, SHE WEIGHED IN AT 8 LBS & 6 OZ. AT 19 INCHES TALL, THE DIMINUTIVE BEAUTY NO LESS TOWERS IN OUR PROUD LITTLE HEARTS.

AVA

GENE MARKS

0620 : **AESTHETIC MOVEMENT** : USA

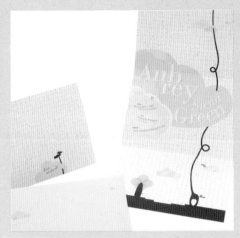

0621 : **SIQUIS** : USA

0622 : **SET EDITIONS** : USA

0623 : **SYNERGY GRAPHIX** : USA

0624 : **SIDESHOW PRESS** : USA

0625 : **ME STUDIO** : THE NETHERLANDS

0626 : **ELEMENTS** : USA

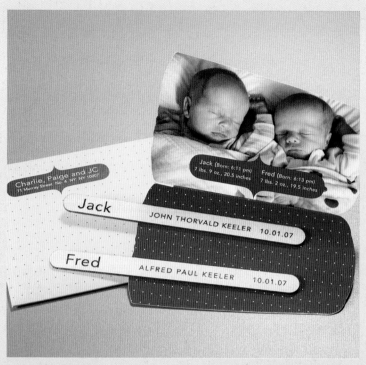

0627 : **VIÑAS DESIGN** : USA

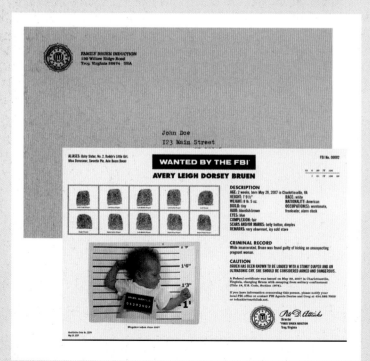

0628 : **CHRIS ROONEY ILLUSTRATION/DESIGN** : USA

0629 : **BEERINBLIK.BE** : BELGIUM

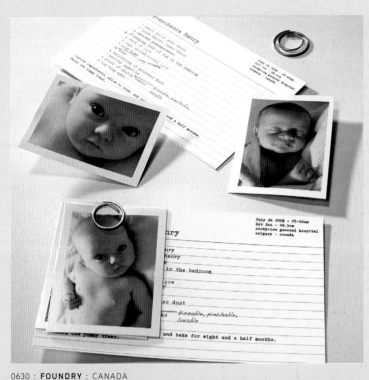

0630 : **FOUNDRY** : CANADA

0631 : **ART SCHOOL GIRL** : USA

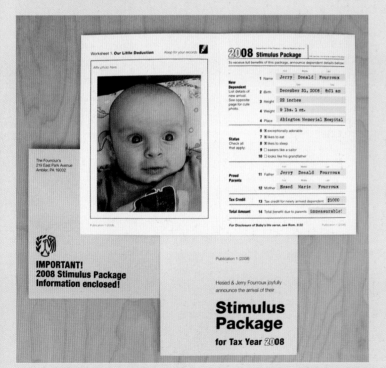

0632 : **CAUSE DESIGN CO.** : USA

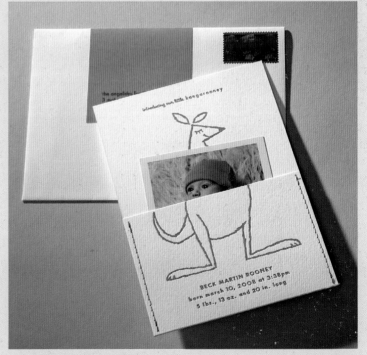

0633 : **CHRIS ROONEY ILLUSTRATION/DESIGN** : USA

0634 : **EVA JANE HOGAN** : IRELAND

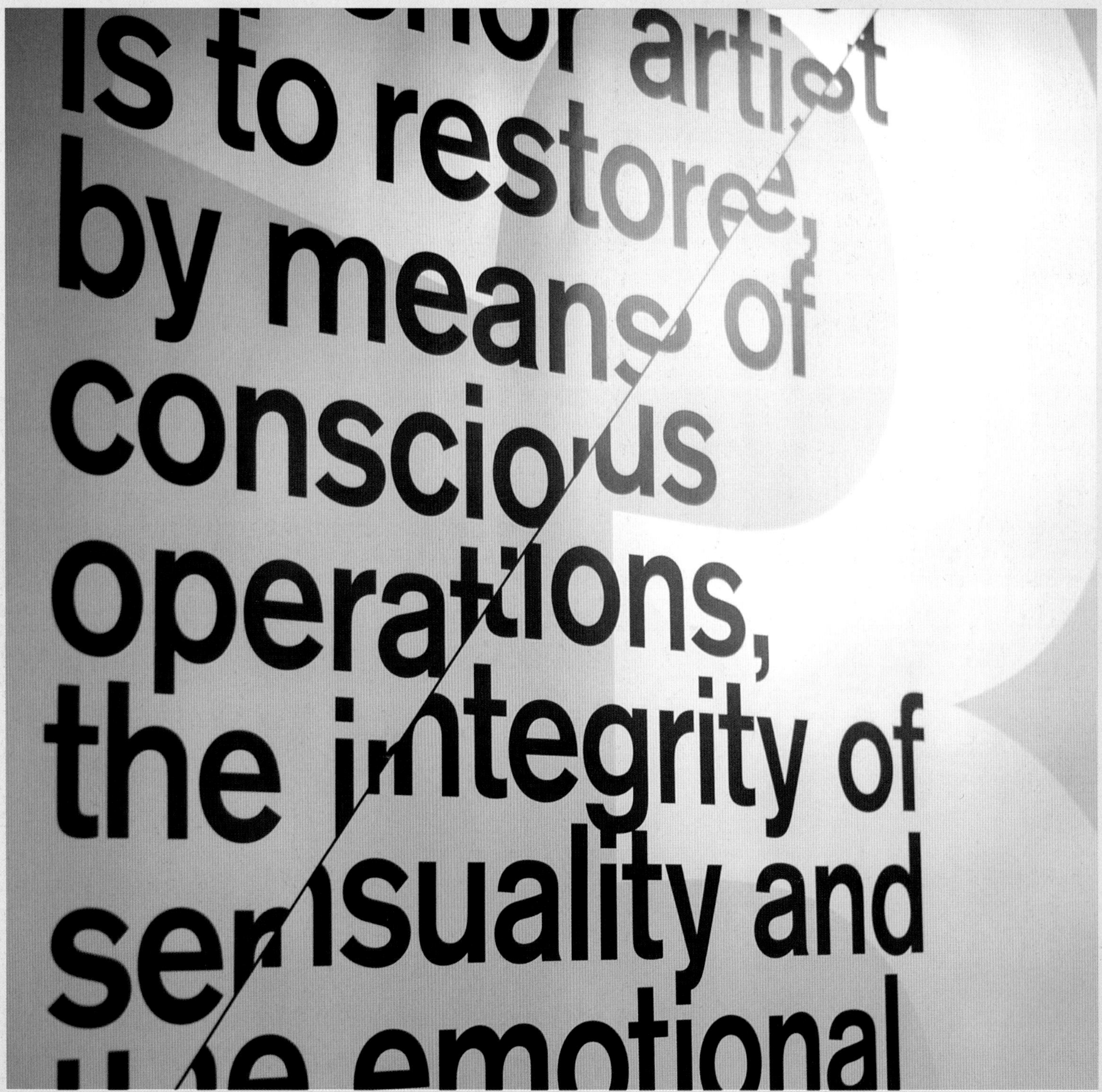

Is to restore,
by means of
conscious
operations,
the integrity of
sensuality and
the emotional

Realize the Imaginary

0637 : **CDRYAN** : USA

Get in here.

0638 : **CDRYAN** : USA

LET YOURSELF GROW

0639 : **CDRYAN** : USA

Support your local Deep Thinker

0640 : **CDRYAN** : USA

STATES UNITED
We The People

0641 : **GREGORY BEAUCHAMP** : USA

ALFABETO
Cosas Que Comienzan Con

0642 : **GREGORY BEAUCHAMP** : USA

ALPHABET
Things That Start With

0643 : **GREGORY BEAUCHAMP** : USA

HOMESTEAD
The Spaces We Return To

0644 : **GREGORY BEAUCHAMP** : USA

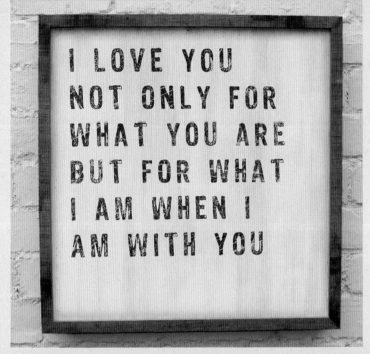

I LOVE YOU
NOT ONLY FOR
WHAT YOU ARE
BUT FOR WHAT
I AM WHEN I
AM WITH YOU

0645 : **COULSON MACLEOD** : UK

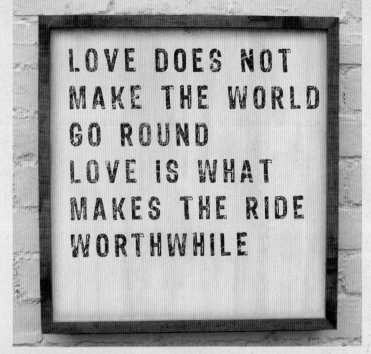

LOVE DOES NOT
MAKE THE WORLD
GO ROUND
LOVE IS WHAT
MAKES THE RIDE
WORTHWHILE

0646 : **COULSON MACLEOD** : UK

AND WHEN
I TOUCH YOU
I FEEL HAPPY
INSIDE

0647 : **COULSON MACLEOD** : UK

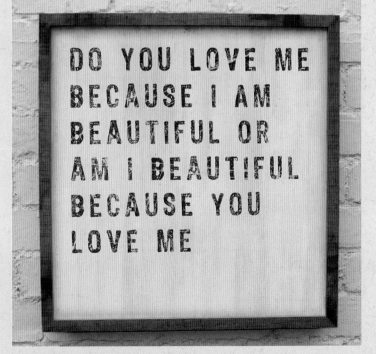

DO YOU LOVE ME
BECAUSE I AM
BEAUTIFUL OR
AM I BEAUTIFUL
BECAUSE YOU
LOVE ME

0648 : **COULSON MACLEOD** : UK

0649 : **DOUG CLOUSE** : USA

0650 : **TOKY BRANDING + DESIGN** : USA

0651 : **EGE SOYUER** : USA

0652 : **EGE SOYUER** : USA

0653 : **TOKY BRANDING + DESIGN** : USA

0654 : **ANAGRAM PRESS** : USA

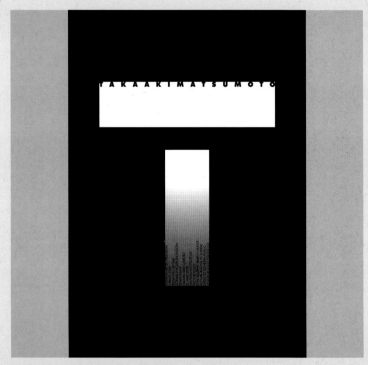

0655 : **PISCATELLO DESIGN CENTRE** : USA

0656 : **PISCATELLO DESIGN CENTRE** : USA

0657 : **JASON BAILEY** : USA

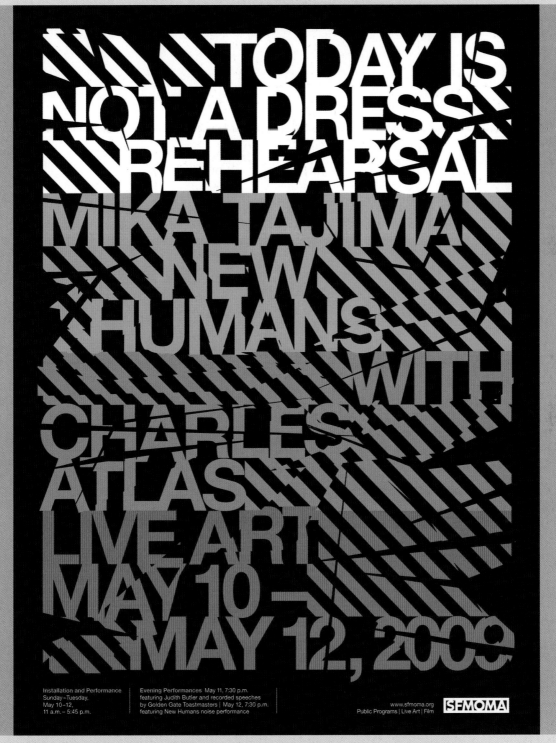

TODAY IS NOT A DRESS REHEARSAL

MIKA TAJIMA NEW HUMANS WITH CHARLES ATLAS LIVE ART MAY 10—MAY 12, 2009

Installation and Performance
Sunday–Tuesday,
May 10–12,
11 a.m. – 5:45 p.m.

Evening Performances May 11, 7:30 p.m.
featuring Judith Butler and recorded speeches
by Golden Gate Toastmasters | May 12, 7:30 p.m.
featuring New Humans noise performance

www.sfmoma.org
Public Programs | Live Art | Film

SFMOMA

0658 : **BOB DINETZ DESIGN** : USA

0660 : **TIMBER DESIGN CO.** : USA

0661 : **TIMBER DESIGN CO.** : USA

0662 : **TIMBER DESIGN CO.** : USA

0663 : **TIMBER DESIGN CO.** : USA

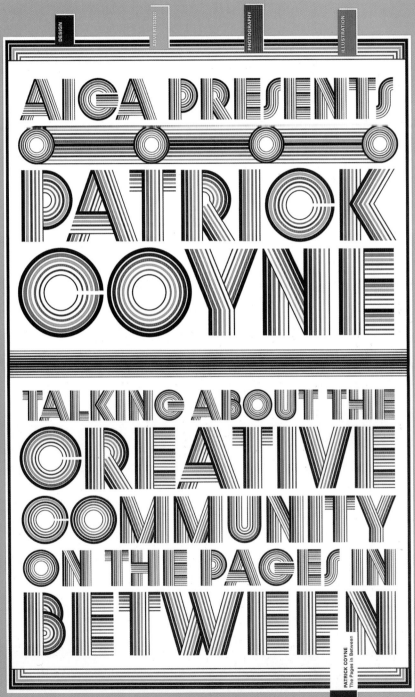

0666 : **MR. FANCY PANTS** : USA

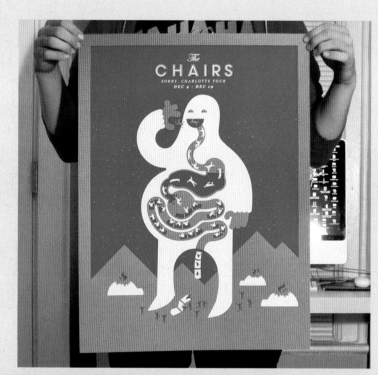

0667 : **BANDITO DESIGN CO** : USA

0668 : **TOKY BRANDING + DESIGN** : USA

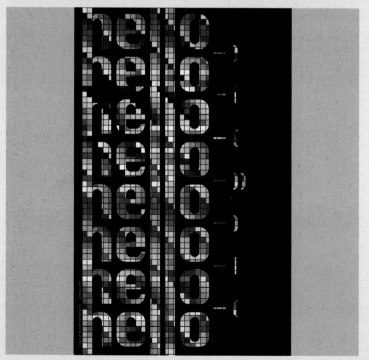

0669 : **WINKBOX.COM** : USA

0670 : **SPLASH PRODUCTIONS PTE LTD** : SINGAPORE

0671 : **SPLASH PRODUCTIONS PTE LTD** : SINGAPORE

0672 : **SPLASH PRODUCTIONS PTE LTD** : SINGAPORE

0673 : **SPLASH PRODUCTIONS PTE LTD** : SINGAPORE

0674 : **INKY LIPS LETTERPRESS** : USA

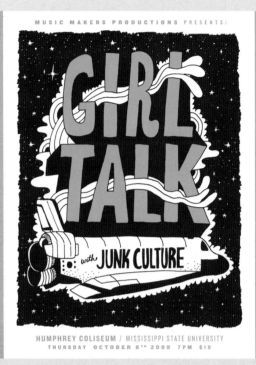

0675 : **MR. FANCY PANTS** : USA

0676 : **GEE + CHUNG DESIGN** : USA

0677 : **INKY LIPS LETTERPRESS** : USA

0678 : **BANDITO DESIGN CO.** : USA   0679 : **DOUG CLOUSE** : USA   0680 : **FOSSIL** : USA

0681 : **BANDITO DESIGN CO.** : USA   0682 : **MY ASSOCIATE CORNELIUS** : USA

0685 : **BENWILSONART.COM** : USA

0686 : **BENWILSONART.COM** : USA

0687 : **BENWILSONART.COM** : USA

0688 : **BENWILSONART.COM** : USA

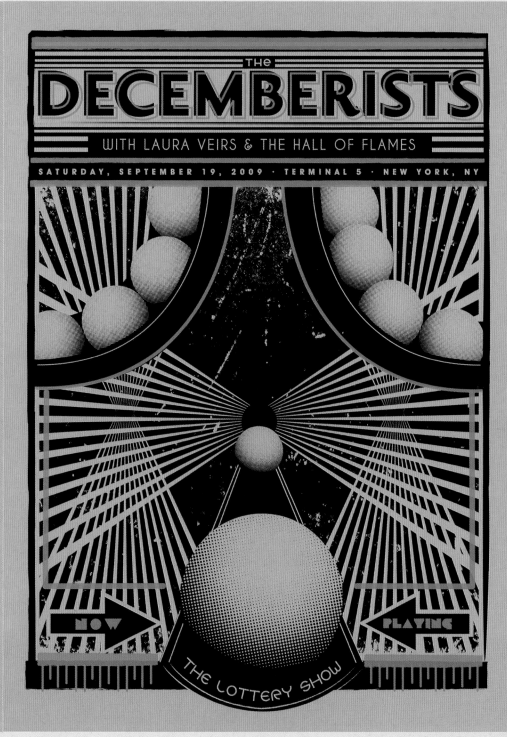

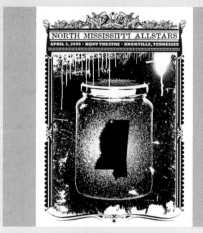

0691 : **STATUS SERIGRAPH** : USA

0692 : **STATUS SERIGRAPH** : USA

0693 : **STATUS SERIGRAPH** : USA

0694 : **STATUS SERIGRAPH** : USA

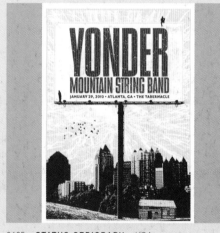

0695 : **STATUS SERIGRAPH** : USA

0696 : **EMORY CASH DESIGN** : USA

0697 : **DOUBLENAUT** : CANADA

0698 : **DOUBLENAUT** : CANADA

0699 : **DOUBLENAUT** : CANADA

The Swell Season

--- JOSH RITTER ---

NOVEMBER 19, 2009

LOS ANGELES THE WILTERN CALIFORNIA

0700 : **DKNG STUDIOS** : USA

WITH **ORISHA** AND **HEALAMONSTER** // JULY 16, 2009 // **SILVERLAKE LOUNGE** LOS ANGELES, CALIFORNIA // **WWW.FIRS.TV**

0701 : **DKNG STUDIOS** : USA

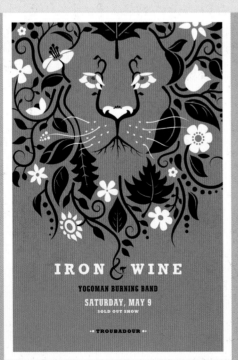

IRON & WINE

YOGOMAN BURNING BAND

SATURDAY, MAY 9

SOLD OUT SHOW

-- TROUBADOUR --

0702 : **DKNG STUDIOS** : USA

The Swell Season

--- JOSH RITTER ---

NOVEMBER 18, 2009

LOS ANGELES THE WILTERN CALIFORNIA

0703 : **DKNG STUDIOS** : USA

0704 : **DKNG STUDIOS** : USA

0705 : **MY ASSOCIATE CORNELIUS** : USA

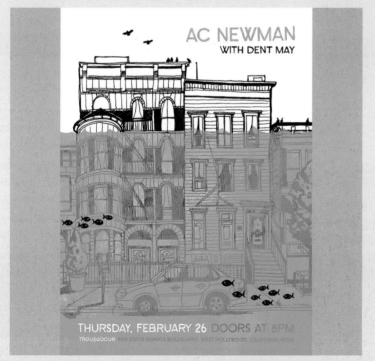

0706 : **DKNG STUDIOS** : USA

0707 : **DKNG STUDIOS** : USA

MYSPACE PRESENTS

METRIC

APRIL 2, 2009
THE GREAT HALL
TORONTO, ON – 9PM

WWW.MYSPACE.COM/SECRETSHOWSCA

0709 : **DOUBLENAUT** : CANADA

0710 : **YEE-HAW INDUSTRIES** : USA

0711 : **EVIN McCORMICK** : USA

0712 : **DKNG STUDIOS** : USA

EXPLOSIONS IN THE SKY with LICHENS • APRIL 9 • STARLIGHT BALLROOM
APRIL 10 • TROCADERO • PHILADELPHIA • ALL AGES

POSTER BY A. MICAH SMITH

0714 : **MY ASSOCIATE CORNELIUS** : USA

0715 : **MY ASSOCIATE CORNELIUS** : USA

0716 : **MY ASSOCIATE CORNELIUS** : USA

0717 : **MY ASSOCIATE CORNELIUS** : USA

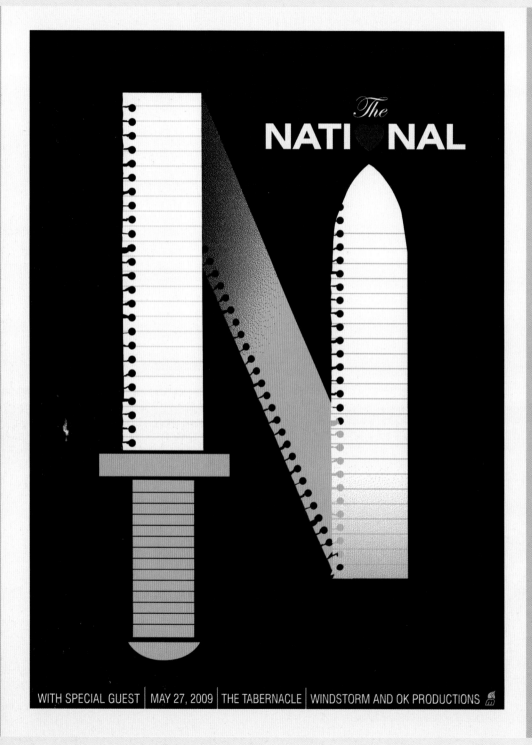

0719 : **METHANE STUDIOS** : USA

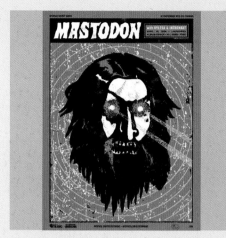

0720 : **MY ASSOCIATE CORNELIUS** : USA

0721 : **MY ASSOCIATE CORNELIUS** : USA

0722 : **MY ASSOCIATE CORNELIUS** : USA

0723 : **MY ASSOCIATE CORNELIUS** : USA

0724 : **MY ASSOCIATE CORNELIUS** : USA

0725 : **TAD CARPENTER/VAHALLA** : USA

0726 : **MY ASSOCIATE CORNELIUS** : USA

0727 : **DKNG STUDIOS** : USA

0728 : **METHANE STUDIOS** : USA

0729 : **MY ASSOCIATE CORNELIUS** : USA

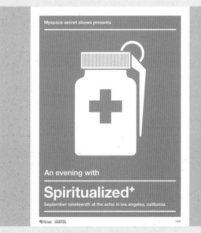

0730 : **MY ASSOCIATE CORNELIUS** : USA

0731 : **MY ASSOCIATE CORNELIUS** : USA

0732 : **MY ASSOCIATE CORNELIUS** : USA

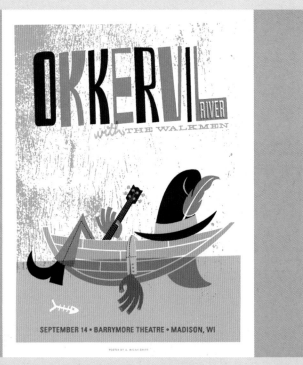

0733 : **MY ASSOCIATE CORNELIUS** : USA

0734 : **MY ASSOCIATE CORNELIUS** : USA

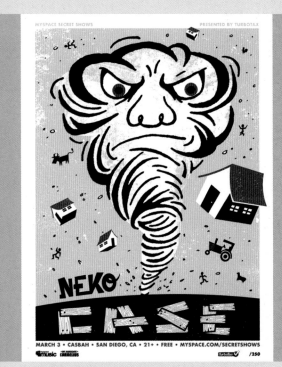

0735 : **MY ASSOCIATE CORNELIUS** : USA

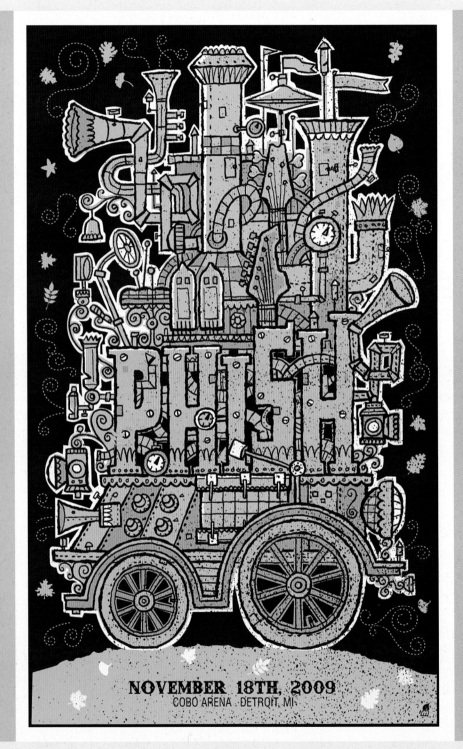

0738 : **METHANE STUDIOS** : USA

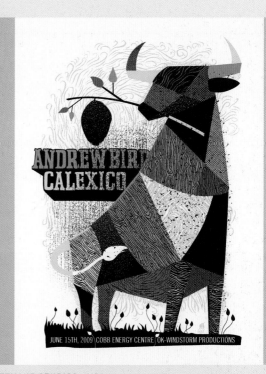

0739 : **METHANE STUDIOS** : USA

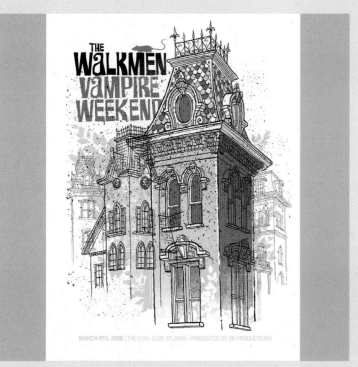

0740 : **METHANE STUDIOS** : USA

0741 : **METHANE STUDIOS** : USA

0742 : **METHANE STUDIOS** : USA

0743 : **METHANE STUDIOS** : USA

0744 : **METHANE STUDIOS** : USA

0745 : **METHANE STUDIOS** : USA

0746 : **METHANE STUDIOS** : USA

0747 : **METHANE STUDIOS** : USA

0748 : **METHANE STUDIOS** : USA

0749 : **METHANE STUDIOS** : USA

0750 : **METHANE STUDIOS** : USA

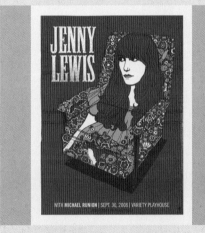

0751 : **METHANE STUDIOS** : USA

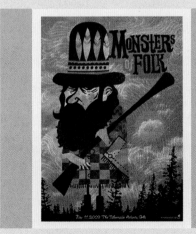

0752 : **METHANE STUDIOS** : USA

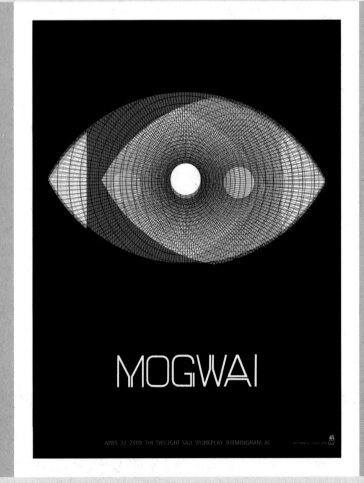

0753 : **METHANE STUDIOS** : USA

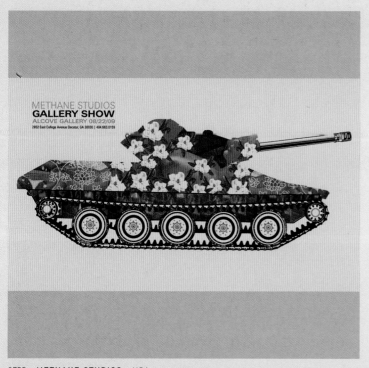

0755 : **METHANE STUDIOS** : USA

0756 : **METHANE STUDIOS** : USA

0757 : **METHANE STUDIOS** : USA

0758 : **MY ASSOCIATE CORNELIUS** : USA

0759 : **TAD CARPENTER/VAHALLA** : USA

0760 : **TAD CARPENTER/VAHALLA** : USA

0761 : **TAD CARPENTER/VAHALLA** : USA

0762 : **TAD CARPENTER/VAHALLA** : USA

MONDAY SEPTEMBER 29 | KANSAS CITY, MISSOURI | UPTOWN THEATER | 8PM

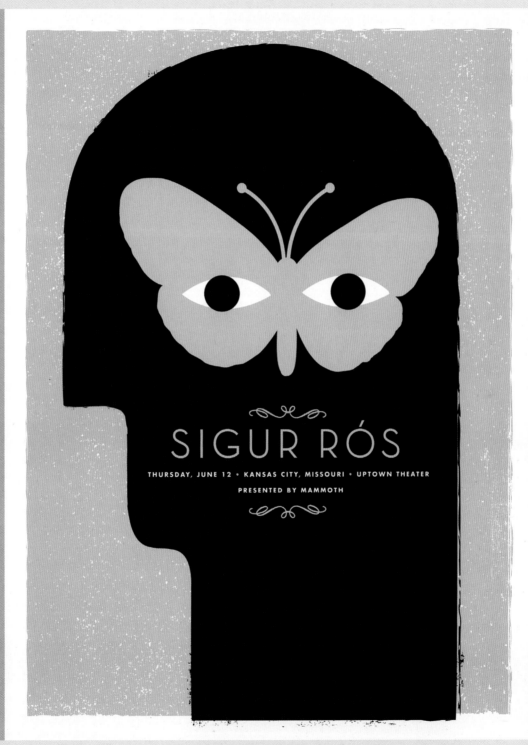

0766 : **TAD CARPENTER**/VAHALLA : USA

0768 : **TAD CARPENTER**/VAHALLA : USA

0767 : **TAD CARPENTER**/VAHALLA : USA

0769 : **TAD CARPENTER**/VAHALLA : USA

0770 : **TAD CARPENTER**/VAHALLA : USA

0771 : **TAD CARPENTER**/VAHALLA : USA

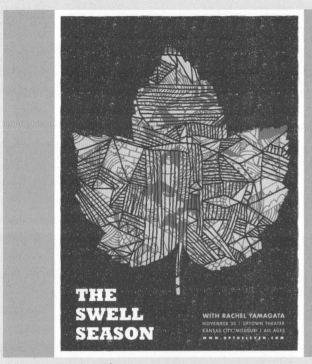

0772 : **TAD CARPENTER**/**VAHALLA** : USA

0773 : **TAD CARPENTER**/**VAHALLA** : USA

0774 : **GARY HOUSTON DESIGN**/**VOODOO CATBOX** : USA

0775 : **GARY HOUSTON DESIGN**/**VOODOO CATBOX** : USA

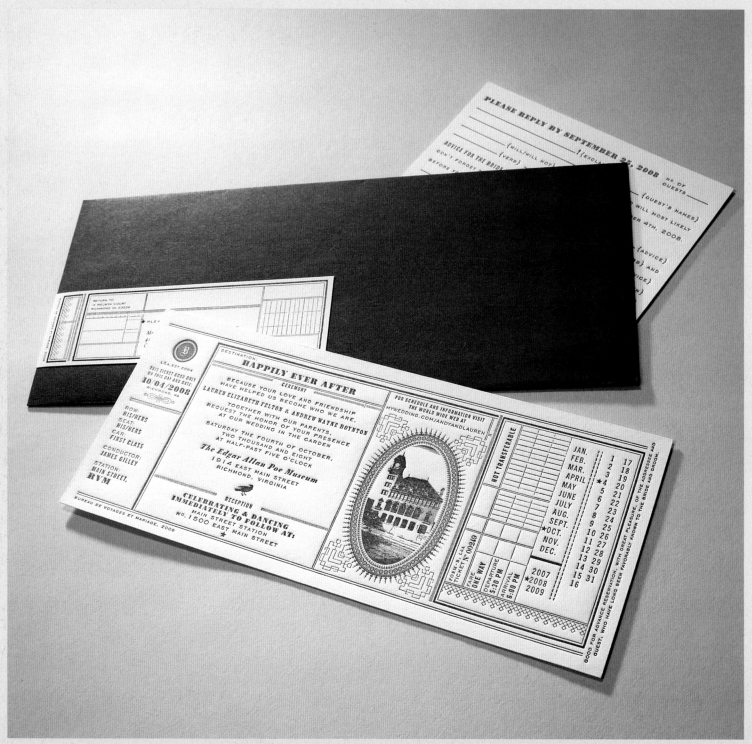

0777 : **KIM CHAN** : USA

0778 : **CREATIVE SQUALL** : USA

0779 : **A3 DESIGN** : USA

0780 : **LAUREN MOON VEDDER** : USA

0781 : **NICEVENTS** : USA

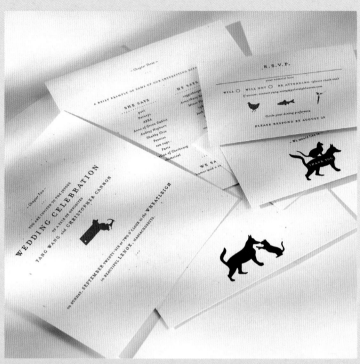

0782 : **ISOTOPE 221** : USA

0783 : **ROOT STUDIO** : UK

0784 : **THE PAPER NUT** : USA

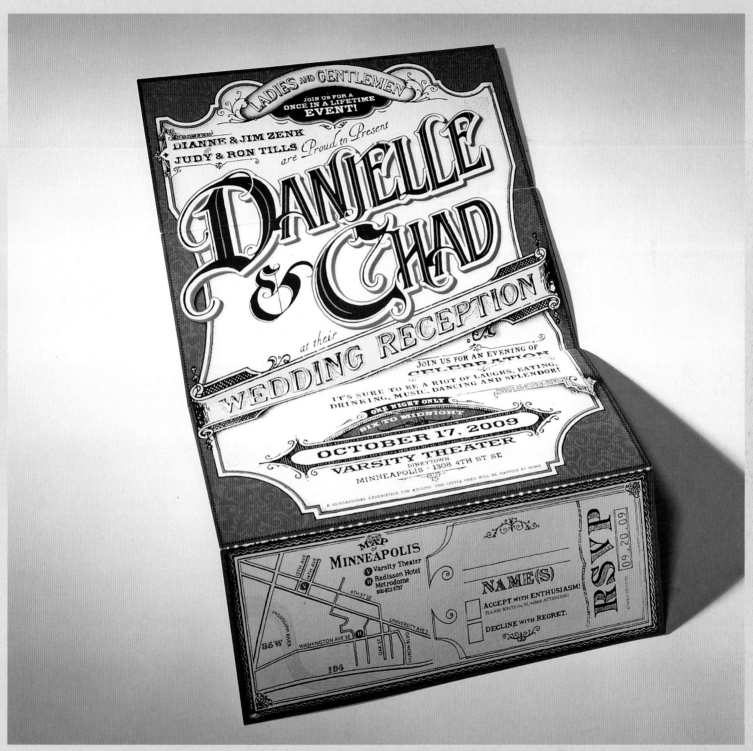

JILL & *MATT*
MET AT WORK.

THOSE WHO WERE THERE WITH THEM KNOW THAT IT WAS AN ODD PLACE TO WORK, BUT JILL NEEDED MONEY FOR GRAD SCHOOL & MATT NEEDED MONEY TO MOVE TO NYC.

THEY GOT ALONG OK.

THEY HAD LUNCH + AFTER-WORK BEERS + BECAME FRIENDS

THEN THE OFFICE CUT EVERYONE'S JOB, SO EVERYONE WENT TO THE BAR.

While at that bar... **SHE** ASKED OUT **HIM.**

He attempted to play coy & nearly blew it.

FOR THE NEXT FOUR MONTHS, they dated the way that normal, sane people date one another

Then, Jill was accepted into grad school in Virginia, & Matt got a job in New York City

AND RIGHT THERE, is where any normality in their courtship came to a halt.

WITHOUT MUCH OF A STRATEGY,

THEY GAVE THE LONG-DISTANCE DATING MODEL A SHOT. (WHICH PROVED TO BE A CRUCIAL LESSON IN PATIENCE).

(LONG STORY SHORT)

IT WENT LIKE THIS FOR TWO FULL YEARS:

Matt visited Jill in Richmond, Virginia.	Jill visited Matt in New York City.

WHEN MATT ASKED:	JILL RESPONDED:
"Why don't you move to New York after school?"	"I love you, but I'm never moving to New York."

(That idea seemed settled)

THEN JILL MOVED TO MAINE FOR A ONE-YEAR RESIDENCY.

THIS WAS EVEN FURTHER AWAY THAN VIRGINIA.

No matter. Matt just trucked up to Maine.	while Jill kept rolling down to New York.

M: "C'mon! Move to NYC with me!" J: "You're very funny. But, no."

AFTER MAINE, JILL LANDED BACK IN PHILLY FOR A YEAR.

CLOSER = BETTER. IT ONLY TOOK THREE YEARS!

New York → VIA GREYHOUND ← **Philadelphia**

Another year + 1/2 passed. One question that kept coming up was *"Do you guys know what you're doing?"*

Ummm...

MATT WAS DIGGING AROUND FOR A SENSIBLE ANSWER WHEN JILL TOLD HIM THAT SHE WAS MOVING TO NEW YORK.

(applause)

Sharing a zip code for the first time in six years, THEY SHARED A LONG-DELAYED REVELATION

THE REVELATION BEING THAT IT TOOK THEM OVER SEVEN YEARS & 48,284 MILES TO ACKNOWLEDGE THAT SOMETIMES, WHEN YOU KNOW, YOU JUST KNOW.

and since that's finally settled...

0791 : **METALMOTHER** : USA

0787 : **OBLATION PAPERS + PRESS** : USA

0788 : **SWEETBEAKER** : USA

0789 : **THRIVE DESIGN** : USA

0790 : **BRIAN BEDNARSKI, CARRIE JONES** : USA

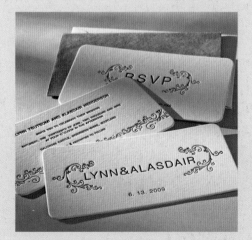

0792 : **AUSTIN PRESS** : USA

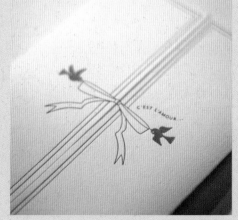

0793 : **THE PAPER NUT** : USA

0795 : **LEAD GRAFFITI** : USA

0794 : **IAN KOENIG** : USA

0796 : **THE PAPER NUT** : USA

0797 : **BLANCA GÓMEZ/COSAS MINIMAS** : SPAIN

0798 : **CACAO DESIGN** : ITALY

0799 : **IAN KOENIG** : USA

0801 : **ALAN VALEK** • **ART DIRECTION + GRAPHIC DESIGN** : USA

0802 : **JOHANN A. GÒMEZ** : USA

0803 : **THREE STEPS AHEAD** : USA

0804 : **MY ASSOCIATE CORNELIUS** : USA

0805 : **RIFLE PAPER CO.** : USA

0806 : **ANONYMOUS ART INC.** : CANADA

0807 : **LEAD GRAFFITI** : USA

0808 : **EMORY CASH DESIGN** : USA

0810 : **INKY LIPS LETTERPRESS** : USA

Ms. Julie Carranzo
146 Scott Street
San Francisco, CA 94117

Donna and Andrew

Mr and Mrs James Kleiber
request the honour of your presence
at the marriage of their daughter

Donna Kleiber
TO
Andrew Clarke
son of
Mr and Mrs Frederick Clarke
Sunday, the eighteenth of October
two thousand nine
at four o'clock in the afternoon
Reception to follow
The Barns at Wesleyan Hills

614 LONG HILL ROAD, MIDDLETOWN, CT
SEMI-FORMAL ATTIRE

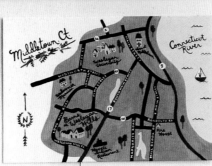

>>> For our guests who are traveling <<<

FROM RT. 9 NORTH or SOUTH
Take Exit 11 (Randolph Road). End of ramp turn left. Follow for
2.2 miles to intersection of Rt. 17 (bottom of steep hill). Turn left onto
Rt. 17 South. Continue on Rt. 17 South until stop light (Cypress Grill on
right) - turn right onto Wesleyan Hills Road. Follow past elementary school,
ponds, barns and around sharp curve and take immediate right into parking lot.

FROM 91 SOUTH
Take Exit 22S (Rt. 9 South, Middletown). Follow directions from Rt. 9 above.

FROM 91 NORTH or MERRIT PKWY
Take Exit for Rt. 66E Middletown (From 91N, Exit 18 - From Rt. 15N, Exit 68
then Exit 18). Stay on Rt. 66 East. At first light (Guida's Drive In), continue
straight 2.5 miles (pass Home Depot on the right). At Walgreens, turn right onto
West Street. At stop sign, go straight over old bridge. Continue straight till end,
at stop sign, turn left onto Wadsworth Street. Take sharp right onto Long Lane off
of Wadsworth St. Follow to end, at stop sign, turn right onto Long Hill Road. Stay
on Long Hill Road around sharp curve, continue to stop sign, go straight. Continue
until just before road curves sharply again, take quick left into parking lot.

FROM the WEST
Take 84 West to 91 South. Follow directions above from 91S.

FOR FURTHER DETAILS, PLEASE VISIT OUR WEDDING SITE:
WWW.THEKNOT.COM/OURWEDDING/DONNAKLEIBERANDREWCLARKE

AIRPORT
Bradley International Airport
Hartford, CT.

AMTRACK TRAIN STATION
Meriden, CT.

HOTELS
Inn at Middletown, Middletown, CT.
Crowne Plaza Cromwell, Cromwell, CT.
Passport Inn & Suites, Middletown, CT.

THINGS TO DO IN TOWN
Never Say Goodbye Antiques & Collectibles
Irreplaceable Artifacts (Demolition Depot)
Kidcity Children's Museum
O'rourke's Diner
Klekolo World Coffee
Wadsworth Mansion at Long Hill Estate

Donna & Andrew
116 N. Water Street
Greenwich, CT
06830

The favor of a reply is requested
by the 25th of September

M_____

— Accepts with pleasure
— Declines with regrets

0812 : **RIFLE PAPER CO.** : USA

0813 : **RIFLE PAPER CO.** : USA

0814 : **RIFLE PAPER CO.** : USA

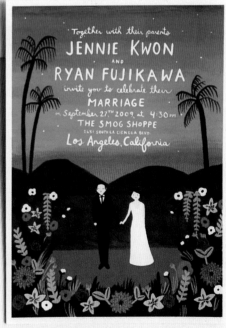

0815 : **RIFLE PAPER CO.** : USA

0816 : **BRODY BOYER** : USA

0817 : **ZEITHEIST PRODUCTIONS** : USA

0818 : **MY ASSOCIATE CORNELIUS** : USA

DR. ROBERT AND SHEILA SEIGEL
INVITE YOU TO CELEBRATE
THE WEDDING OF THEIR DAUGHTER

Amy Lin

TO

Jonathan Ward Engle

JOIN THEM ON THE HIGH DESERT MESA OF SANTA FE
SATURDAY, THE THIRD OF OCTOBER
TWO THOUSAND AND NINE
FOUR O'CLOCK IN THE AFTERNOON

TO RSVP AND FOR ADDITIONAL EVENT
DETAILS INCLUDING TRAVEL INFORMATION,
PLEASE VISIT OUR WEBSITE AT:
AMYANDJONATHAN.WEDDINGWINDOW.COM

I'LL LOVE YOU, DEAR, I'LL LOVE YOU
TILL CHINA AND AFRICA MEET
AND THE RIVER JUMPS OVER THE MOUNTAIN
AND THE SALMON SING IN THE STREET.
W. H. Auden

0820 : **ORANGE SPOT PINK NOSE** : USA

0821 : **ELEVATED PRESS** : USA

0822 : **JANE HANCOCK PAPERS** : USA

0823 : **GREENWICH LETTERPRESS** : USA

SAVE THE DATE

SEVENTEEN OF JULY TWO THOUSAND TEN

VERY HAPPY NEWS

Charlotte Wright
AND
Oliver Ross

invite ... their joy

Saturday, se... ...ousand ten
three ... ...on at
St. ... ...al
200 Church ... ...to, Ontario

wedding banquet to be held at
The Fairmont Royal York
100 Front Street West, Toronto, Ontario

cocktail served at six in the evening
reception at seven

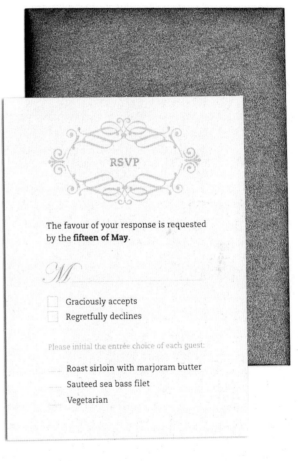

RSVP

The favour of your response is requested
by the **fifteen of May**.

M _____

☐ Graciously accepts
☐ Regretfully declines

Please initial the entrée choice of each guest:

___ Roast sirloin with marjoram butter

___ Sauteed sea bass filet

___ Vegetarian

0825 : **DESIGN DES TROY** : USA

0826 : **SIDESHOW PRESS** : USA

0827 : **SIDESHOW PRESS** : USA

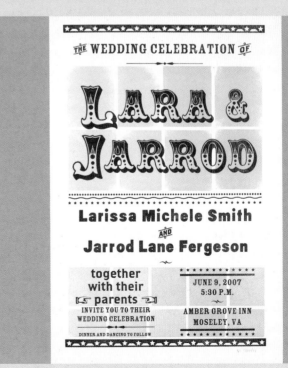

0828 : **INKY LIPS LETTERPRESS** : USA

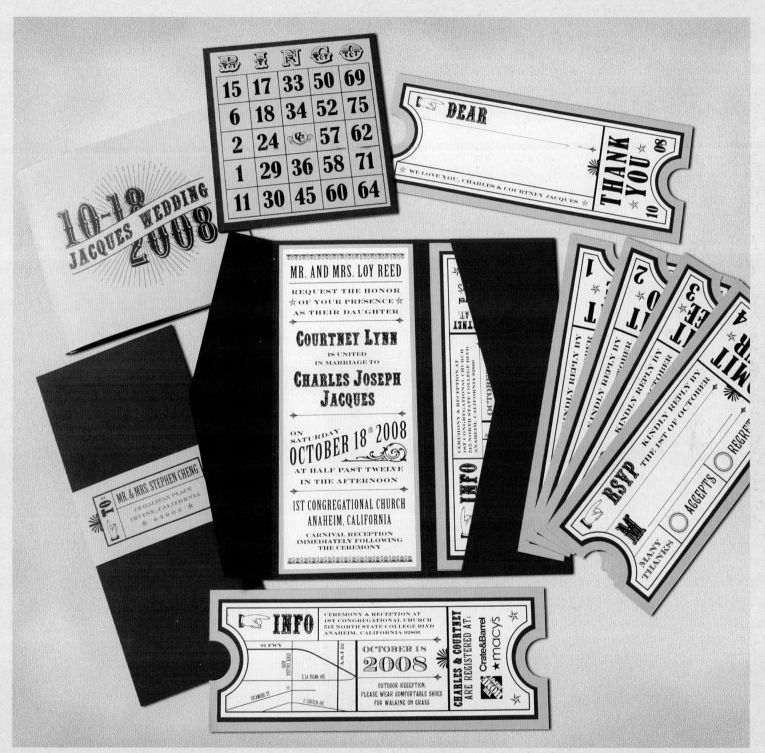

0830 : **OH JOY!** : USA

0831 : **KATHERINE AHN** : USA

0832 : **KATHERINE AHN** : USA

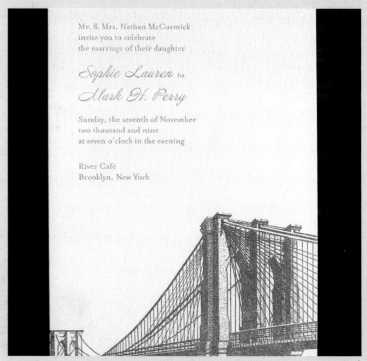

0833 : **GREENWICH LETTERPRESS** : USA

0834 : **KIRTLAND HOUSE PRESS** : USA

0835 : **DAVID SENIOR** : USA

0836 : **DAVID SENIOR** : USA

0837 : **GREENWICH LETTERPRESS** : USA

0840 : **BROWN SUGAR DESIGN** : USA

0839 : **M-ART** : USA

0841 : **HEARTS & ANCHORS** : USA

0842 : **LEAD GRAFFITI** : USA

0843 : **RECHERCHÉ INVITATIONS** : USA

0844 : **NATOOF** : UAE

0845 : **HELEN LAI** : CANADA

0846 : **RECHERCHÉ INVITATIONS** : USA

0847 : **ERIN BAZOS** : USA

0848 : **NICEVENTS** : USA

0849 : **ELEVATED PRESS** : USA

0850 : **ELEVATED PRESS** : USA

0851 : **PANCAKES & FRANKS** : USA

0852 : **NICEVENTS** : USA

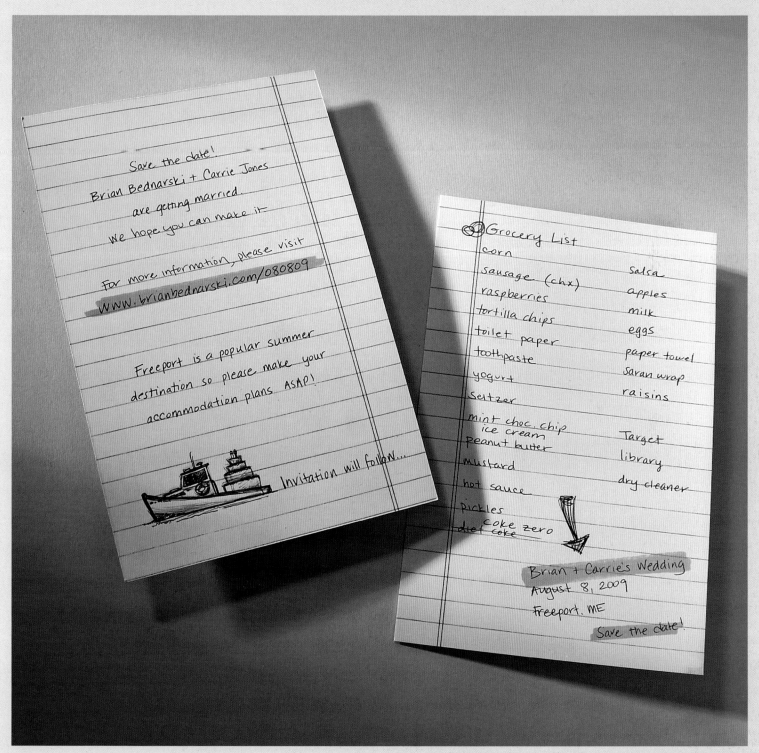

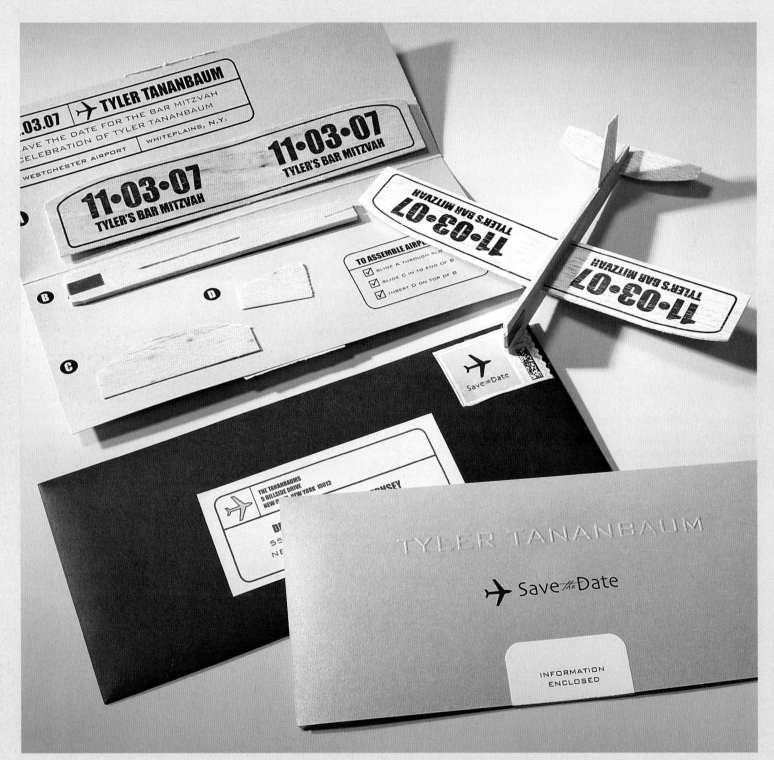

0855 : **ORANGEBEAUTIFUL** : USA

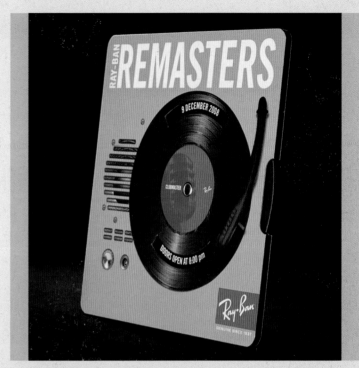

0856 : **CACAO DESIGN** : ITALY

0857 : **CACAO DESIGN** : ITALY

0858 : **SAINT BERNADINE MISSION** : CANADA

0859 : **GUTIERREZ DESIGN ASSOCIATES** : USA

0860 : **KIRTLAND HOUSE PRESS** : USA

0861 : **42INK DESIGN** : CANADA

0862 : **INKY LIPS LETTERPRESS** : USA

0863 : **JANE HANCOCK PAPERS** : USA

0864 : **TIMBER DESIGN CO.** : USA

0865 : **VIÑAS DESIGN** : USA

0868 : **LILLY & LOUISE** : USA

0866 : **INKY LIPS LETTERPRESS** : USA

0867 : **SIDESHOW PRESS** : USA

0870 : **GREENLIGHT DESIGNS** : USA

0871 : **GREENLIGHT DESIGNS** : USA

0872 : **MINDSEYE CREATIVE** : INDIA

0873 : **SK+G ADVERTISING** : USA

0874 : **IRIS A. BROWN DESIGN LLC** : USA

0875 : **ALEX PARROTT** : UK

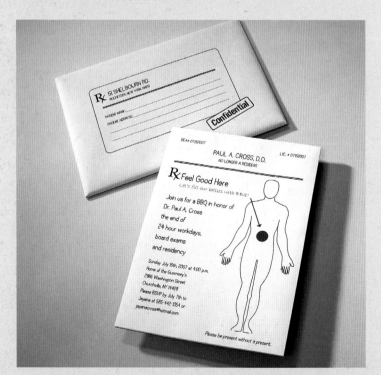

0876 : **SHAUNA CROSS DESIGN** : USA

0877 : **TIMBER DESIGN CO.** : USA

0882 : **SIDESHOW PRESS** : USA

0883 : **SIDESHOW PRESS** : USA

0884 : **SIDESHOW PRESS** : USA

0885 : **SIDESHOW PRESS** : USA

0886 : **ORANGE SPOT PINK NOSE** : USA

0887 : **SK+G ADVERTISING** : USA

0888 : **CARMEDIA DESIGN** : USA

0889 : **EXPLORARE** : MEXICO

0891 : **ANOTHER LIMITED REBELLION** : USA

0892 : **THE JONES GROUP** : USA

0893 : **JUICEBOX DESIGNS** : USA

0894 : **RIPPLE MARKETING** : USA

0895 : **ANOTHER LIMITED REBELLION** : USA

0896 : **ATOMIC DUST** : USA

0897 : **IRIS A. BROWN DESIGN LLC** : USA

0898 : **ATOMIC DUST** : USA

0899 : **SIDESHOW PRESS** : USA

0900 : **DONNA KARAN IN-HOUSE** : USA

0901 : **SIDESHOW PRESS** : USA

0902 : **DONNA KARAN IN-HOUSE** : USA

0903 : **SIDESHOW PRESS** : USA

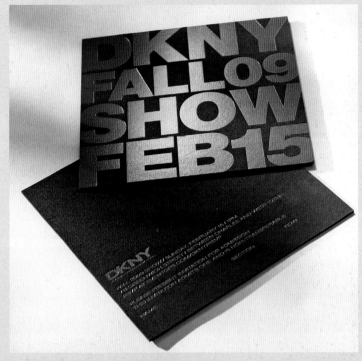

0904 : **DONNA KARAN IN-HOUSE** : USA

0905 : **SIDESHOW PRESS** : USA

0906 : **MICHAEL OSBORNE DESIGN** : USA

0909 : **ANTHROPOLOGIE** : USA

0910 : **TOKY BRANDING + DESIGN** : USA

0911 : **ADD** : USA

0912 : **ANTHROPOLOGIE** : USA

0914 : **BBMG** : USA

0915 : **TOKY BRANDING + DESIGN** : USA

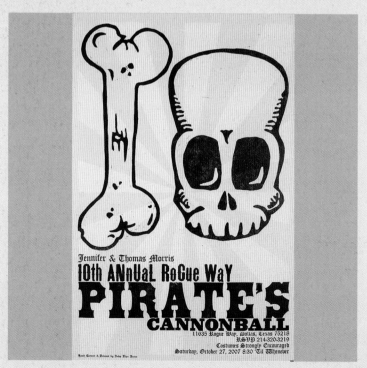

0916 : **INKY LIPS LETTERPRESS** : USA

0917 : **LODGE** : USA

0918 : **A3 DESIGN** : USA

0919 : **GILAH PRESS + DESIGN** : USA

0920 : **BROWN SUGAR DESIGN** : USA

0921 : **UGLY DUCKLING PRESS** : USA

0922 : **TIMBER DESIGN CO.** : USA

0923 : **UGLY DUCKLING PRESS** : USA

0925 : **TIMBER DESIGN CO.** : USA

0926 : **JULIA REICH DESIGN** : USA

0927 : **GRETEMAN GROUP** : USA

0928 : **SELTZER DESIGN** : USA

0929 : **SIDESHOW PRESS** : USA

0934 : **IMAGINE** : UK

0930 : **AERAKI** : GREECE

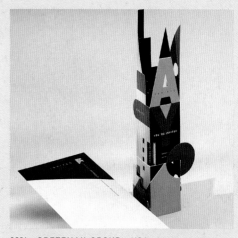

0931 : **GRETEMAN GROUP** : USA

0932 : **SK+G** : USA

0933 : **AERAKI** : GREECE

0935 : **GEE + CHUNG DESIGN** : USA

0936 : **GEE + CHUNG DESIGN** : USA

0937 : **HA DESIGN** : USA

0938 : **THE NBC AGENCY** : USA

0939 : **FOUNDRY** : CANADA

0940 : **TIMBER DESIGN CO.** : USA

0941 : **ALEXANDER EGGER** : AUSTRIA

0942 : **GERARD DESIGN** : USA

0943 : **REICH + PETCH** : CANADA

0944 : **BARNHART** : USA

0945 : **THE CREATIVE METHOD** : AUSTRALIA

0946 : **SK+G ADVERTISING** : USA

0947 : **WALLACE CHURCH, INC.** : USA

0948 : **160OVER90** : USA

0949 : **THE CREATIVE METHOD** : AUSTRALIA

0950 : **GEE + CHUNG DESIGN** : USA

0951 : **WWW.CACAODESIGN.IT** : ITALY

0952 : **C3 – CREATIVE CONSUMER CONCEPTS** : USA

0953 : **SIDESHOW PRESS** : USA

0954 : **GEE + CHUNG DESIGN** : USA

0955 : **C3 – CREATIVE CONSUMER CONCEPTS** : USA

0956 : **DAVID CLARK DESIGN** : USA

0957 : **UBER** : UK

0958 : **UBER** : UK

0959 : **DEAN JAMES BALLAS** : USA

0961 : **SK+G ADVERTISING** : USA

0962 : **GREENLIGHT DESIGNS** : USA

0963 : **MINDSEYE CREATIVE** : INDIA

0964 : **GREENLIGHT DESIGNS** : USA

0965 : **SK+G** : USA

0966 : **SK+G** : USA

0967 : **MINDSEYE CREATIVE** : INDIA

0968 : **SERAPH DESIGN** : USA

0969 : **OBERLANDER GROUP** : USA

0970 : **SK+G** : USA

0971 : **LEAD GRAFFITI** : USA

At Greenlight Designs we like to think that we put our flesh and blood into every project. We like to nail a campaign by knuckling under, cutting to the chase, bringing something to life and showing you a little piece of ourselves. So give us a call (818) 509-0787. Chop, chop!

0972 : **GREENLIGHT DESIGNS** : USA

0973 : **JOEY'S CORNER** : USA

0974 : **SIDESHOW PRESS** : USA

0975 : **ANOTHER LIMITED REBELLION** : USA

0976 : **ZINNOBERGRUEN GMBH** : GERMANY

0977 : **VIÑAS DESIGN** : USA

0978 : **ANOTHER LIMITED REBELLION** : USA

0979 : **WALLACE CHURCH, INC.** : USA

0980 : **SYNERGY GRAPHIX** : USA

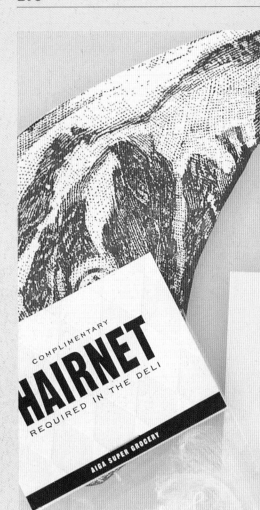

COMPLIMENTARY

HAIRNET

REQUIRED IN THE DELI

AIGA SUPER GROCERY

EMPLOYEE
OF THE MONTH
INSHOW 15

PARTY ON

South Carolina's

YOU'RE INVITED

GA

INSHOW GALA
11/6/09 7–9 p.m.
701 Whaley Street
Columbia, SC

GALA EXTRA: At the event,
AIGA will be collecting
canned goods for Harvest
Hope Food Bank. Bring a can
or two if you can!

GALA PRINT & SWAG BY:
Stitch Design Co.
Sideshow Press
Sandy Lang, Writer
Wentworth Printing

 South Carolina

15TH ANNUAL INSHOW
inshow-o-rama.com special

SHELVES STOCKED ONLY WITH
THE BRANDS AND ENTRIES
THAT MADE IT **IN.**

7-9 P.M. FRIDAY, NOVEMBER 6, 2009

FREE FOR AIGA MEMBERS
NON-MEMBERS $40 ★ STUDENT NON-MEMBERS $20

701 Whaley Street, Columbia, SC

RSVP BY 11/2/09 TO INSHOW@SOUTHCAROLINA.AIGA.ORG

0982 : **SEVEN25. DESIGN & TYPOGRAPHY** : CANADA

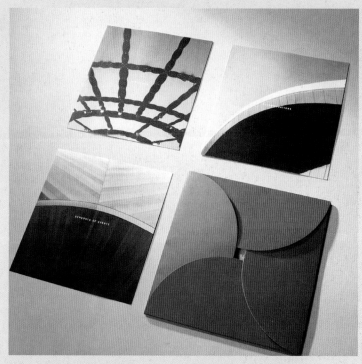

0983 : **OBERLANDER GROUP** : USA

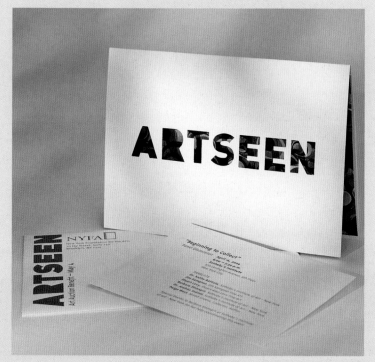

0984 : **ANOTHER LIMITED REBELLION** : USA

0985 : **WALLACE CHURCH, INC.** : USA

0987 : **TOKY BRANDING + DESIGN** : USA

0988 : **LODGE** : USA

0989 : **ZYNC** : CANADA

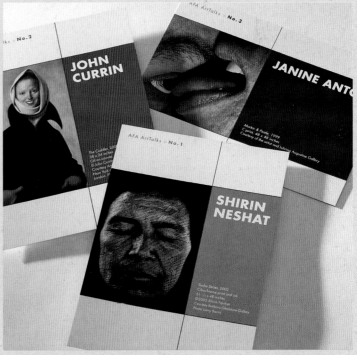

0990 : **GOODESIGN** : USA

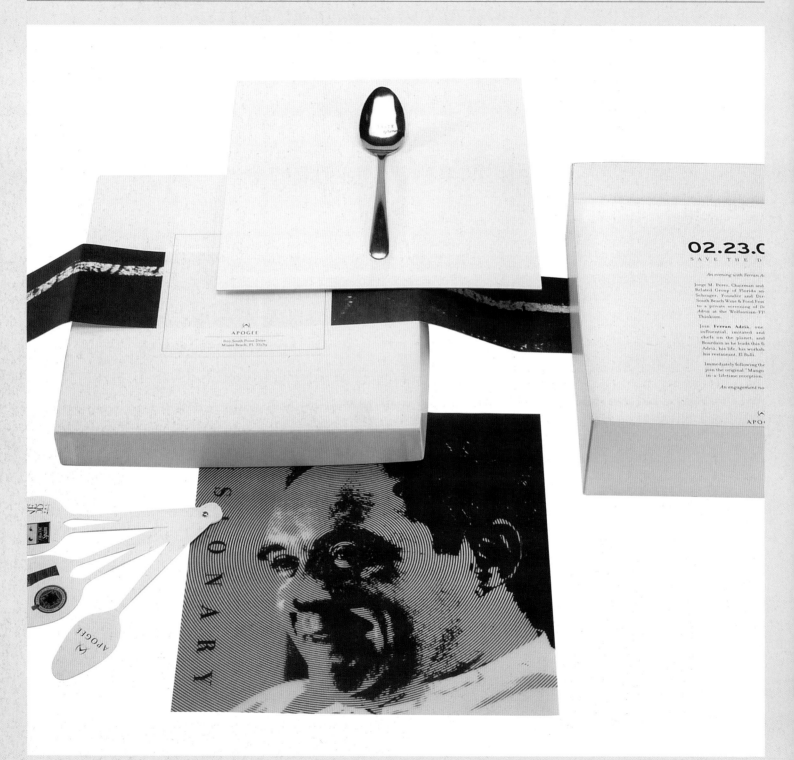

0992 : **CACAO DESIGN** : ITALY

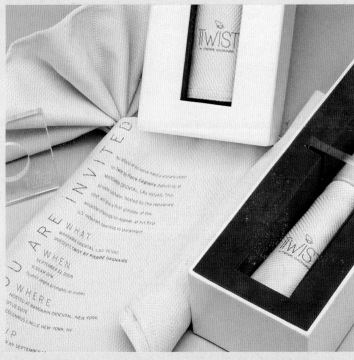

0993 : **SK+G** : USA

0994 : **SK+G** : USA

0995 : **SERAPH DESIGN** : USA

0996 : **SIDESHOW PRESS** : USA

0997 : **TOKY BRANDING + DESIGN** : USA

0998 : **BERGWORKS GBM** : USA

0999 : **KIM KNOLL** : USA

DIRECTORY

>PROMPTT
49 MISSOURI ST., #10
SAN FRANCISCO, CA 94107
USA
415-431-4173
CORRINE@PROMPTT.COM

0408, 0409
DESIGNER: Corrine Morita
CLIENT: Self

160VER90
1 SOUTH BROAD ST., FLOOR 10
PHILADELPHIA, PA 19107
USA
215-732-3200
MPRESCOTT@160OVER90.COM
WWW.160OVER90.COM

0560
ART DIRECTOR: Darryl Cilli
DESIGNER: Adam Flanagan,
Stephen Penning
CLIENT: 160over90

0948
ART DIRECTOR: Stephen Penning
DESIGNER: Mikey Burton
CLIENT: 160over90

42INK DESIGN
714 GERRARD ST. E.
TORONTO, ONTARIO M4M 1Y3
CANADA
416-889-9442
KIRSTIN@42INK.COM
WWW.42INK.COM

0861
ART DIRECTOR: Kirstin Thomas
DESIGNER: Kirstin Thomas
CLIENT: Personal

A3 DESIGN
PO BOX 37
WEBSTER, NY 14580
USA
704-562-9108
AMANDA@A3-DESIGN.COM
WWW.A3-DESIGN.COM

0515
ART DIRECTOR: Amanda Altman
DESIGNER: Alan Altman, Gina Hayes
CLIENT: A3 Design

0665
ART DIRECTOR: Amanda Altman
DESIGNER: Alan Altman, Gina Hayes
CLIENT: AIGA Charlotte, NC

0779
ART DIRECTOR: Amanda Altman
DESIGNER: Alan Altman
CLIENT: Michael Florin

0918
ART DIRECTOR: Amanda Altman
DESIGNER: Alan Altman
CLIENT: "Turbo" Mike Florin

ACME INDUSTRIES
I COANEI 98
BUCHAREST
ROMANIA
0040 744 304 886
ANDREI.ROBU@GMAIL.COM
WWW.ANDREIROBU.COM

0414
ART DIRECTOR: Andrei D. Robu
DESIGNER: Andrei D. Robu

ADD
120 N. 7TH ST., #4B
BROOKLYN, NY 11211
USA
646-327-6585
DESIGN@ADD-NY.COM
WWW.ADD-NY.COM

0484
DESIGNER: Erin Bazos
CLIENT: Datagraphic

0911
DESIGNER: Erin Bazos
CLIENT: Hugo Boss

AERAKI
47, TROIAS ST.
11251 ATHENS
GREECE
30 210 88 21 960
INFO@AERAKI.GR
WWW.AERAKI.GR

0529, 0930, 0933
ART DIRECTOR: Despina Aeraki
DESIGNER: Despina Aeraki
CLIENT: Self

AESTHETIC MOVEMENT
(FORMERLY GOODESIGN)
9-20 35TH AVE., #3F
LONG ISLAND CITY, NY 11106
USA
718-797-5750
DIANE@AESTHETICMOVEMENT.COM
WWW.AESTHETICMOVEMENT.COM

0477
DESIGNER: Diane Shaw
CLIENT: Robin Hood Foundation

0478, 0521
ART DIRECTOR: Diane Shaw
DESIGNER: Jennifer Blanco
CLIENT: Robin Hood Foundation

0521
DESIGNERS: Diane Shaw,
Kathryn Hammill
CLIENT: In-House

0579
DESIGNERS: Diane Shaw,
Kathryn Hammill
CLIENT: Lava

0608
DESIGNER: Diane Shaw
CLIENT: NBC Universal

0610
DESIGNER: Diane Shaw,
Kathryn Hammill
CLIENT: World Studio Foundation

0620
DESIGNER: Jesse James
PRINTER: Austin Press

0664
ART DIRECTOR: Kathryn Hammill
CLIENT: Brooklyn Arts Council

0990
DESIGNER: Kathryn Hammill
CLIENT: American Federation
of Art

ALAN VALEK • ART DIRECTION +
GRAPHIC DESIGN
767 EUCLID AVE., #14
LONG BEACH, CA 90804
USA
714-488-3728
INFO@ALANVALEK.COM
WWW.ALANVALEK.COM

0494, 0801
ART DIRECTOR: Alan Valek
DESIGNER: Slan Valek
CLIENT: Self

ALEX PARROTT
EVA COTTAGES, 13 CAMP RD.
ST. ALBANS, HERTFORDSHIRE
AL1 5DX
UK
44 (0)7951 966656
ALEX@ALEXPARROTT.CO.UK
WWW.ALEXPARROTT.CO.UK

0506, 0875
DESIGNER: Alex Parrott
CLIENT: Terra Firma

ALEXANDER EGGER
HORNECKGASSE 8/6
7770 VIENNA
AUSTRIA
ALEX@SATELLITESMISTAKENFOR
STARS.COM
WWW.SATELLITESMISTAKENFOR
STARS.COM

0941
ART DIRECTOR: Alexander Egger
DESIGNER: Alexander Egger
CLIENT: Pilot Projekt

AMBER JOSEY
1112 E. 10TH ST., APT 1E
GREENVILLE, NC 27858
USA
828-781-9225
ADJO126@ECU.EDU

0527
DESIGNER: Amber Josey

ANAGRAM PRESS
PO BOX 7443
TACOMA, WA 98417
USA
253-310-8770
CHANDLER@ANAGRAM-PRESS.COM
WWW.ANAGRAM-PRESS.COM

0654
ART DIRECTOR: Chandler O'Leary
DESIGNER: Chandler O'Leary
CLIENT: Anagram Press

ANAGRAM PRESS & IGLOO
LETTERPRESS
PO BOX 7443
TACOMA, WA 98417
USA
253-310-8770
CHANDLER@ANAGRAM-PRESS.COM
WWW.ANAGRAM-PRESS.COM

0167
ART DIRECTOR: Allison Chapman
DESIGNER: Chandler O'Leary
CLIENT: Anagram Press & Igloo
Letterpress
LETTERPRESS PRINTER: Allison
Chapman

0169, 0374
ART DIRECTOR: Allison Chapman
DESIGNER: Chandler O'Leary
CLIENT: Collaboration with Igloo
Letterpress
LETTERPRESS PRINTER: Allison
Chapman

ANAGRAM PRESS & SPRINGTIDE
PRESS
PO BOX 7443
TACOMA, WA 98417
USA
253-310-8770
CHANDLER@ANAGRAM-PRESS.COM
WWW.ANAGRAM-PRESS.COM

0522 – 0524
ART DIRECTOR: Jessica Spring
DESIGNER: Chandler O'Leary
CLIENT: Fine Art Collaboration
with Jessica Spring
LETTERPRESS PRINTER: Jessica
Spring

ANDY BABB
PO BOX 6
LINCOLN, VA 20160
USA
540-454-0719
ANDY@ANDYBABB.COM
WWW.ANDYBABB.COM

0569
ART DIRECTOR: Andy Babb
DESIGNER: Andy Babb
CLIENT: Self

ANDY PRATT DESIGN
203 E. 4TH ST., #9
NEW YORK, NY 10009
USA
646-379-0081
HELLO@ANDYPRATT.NET
WWW.ANDYPRATT.NET

0086 – 0089, 0101 – 0109,

0200, 0201, 0240, 0241, 0243,

0526
ART DIRECTOR: Andy Pratt
CLIENT: Andy Pratt

ANONYMOUS ART INC.
213 MICHIGAN ST.
VICTORIA, BC
CANADA
250-704-0456
REBECCA@ANONYMOUSART.CA
WWW.ANONYMOUSART.CA

0806
ART DIRECTOR: Rebecca Gerein
DESIGNER: Karen Yen, Rebecca
Gerein
CLIENT: Amanda & Jason

ANOTHER LIMITED REBELLION
2701 EDGEWOOD AVE.
RICHMOND, VA 23222
USA
804-321-6677
CONTACT@ALRDESIGN.COM
WWW.ALRDESIGN.COM

0891
ART DIRECTOR: Noah Scanlin
DESIGNER: Noah Scanlin
CLIENT: Target Margin Theater

0895
ART DIRECTOR: Noah Scanlin
DESIGNER: Noah Scanlin
CLIENT: Vizual Entertainment

0975, 0978
ART DIRECTOR: Noah Scanlin
DESIGNER: Noah Scanlin
CLIENT: Bang on a Can

0984
ART DIRECTOR: Noah Scanlin
DESIGNER: Noah Scanlin
CLIENT: New York Foundation for
the Arts

ANTHROPOLOGIE
5000 S. BROAD ST., BUILDING 10
PHILADELPHIA, PA
USA
KFABRIZIO@ANTHROPOLOGIE.COM

0907
ART DIRECTOR: Carolyn Keer
CLIENT: In-House

0908
ART DIRECTOR: Carolyn Keer
DESIGNER: Alana Mccann, Lizania
Cruz
CLIENT: In-House

0909
ART DIRECTOR: Carolyn Keer
DESIGNER: Alana Mccann
CLIENT: In-House

0912
ART DIRECTOR: Carolyn Keer
DESIGNER: Kate Fabrizio
CLIENT: In-House

**ANVIL GRAPHIC DESIGN DBA
ANVIL MODERN PAPERIE**
65 EL VANADA RD.
REDWOOD CITY, CA 94062
USA
650-261-6090
SUPPORT@HITANVIL.COM
WWW.ANVILPAPER.COM;
WWW.CARDSTORE.COM

0318 – 0321
ART DIRECTOR: Laura Bauer
DESIGNER: Laura Bauer
CLIENT: cardstore.com

ART SCHOOL GIRL
2554 W WILSON AVE., #1
CHICAGO, IL 60625
USA
773-405-0219
AMY@ARTSCHOOLGIRL.COM
WWW.ARTSCHOOLGIRL.COM

0024
ART DIRECTOR: Amy Rowan
DESIGNER: Amy Rowan
ILLUSTRATION: Ryan Thurlwell

**0064, 0066, 0116, 0117, 0138,
0139, 0141, 0171, 0509, 0512,
0631**
ART DIRECTOR: Amy Rowan
DESIGNER: Amy Rowan

0140
ART DIRECTOR: Amy Rowan
DESIGNER: Amy Rowan
ILLUSTRATION: Denise Holmes

ATOMIC DUST
317 N. 11TH ST., SUITE 300
ST. LOUIS, MO 63101
USA
314-241-2866
MROESER@ATOMICDUST.COM
WWW.ATOMICDUST.COM

0517 – 0520
ART DIRECTOR: Mike Spakowski
DESIGNER: Matt Roeser
CLIENT: Atomic Dust

0537 – 0539, 0896, 0898
ART DIRECTOR: Mike Spakowski
DESIGNER: Katie Werges
CLIENT: Atomic Dust

AUSTIN PRESS
USA
KIM@KIMATT.NET

0076 – 0079, 0081, 0792

AYA IKEGAYA
102 PRINCE ST., #4
NEW YORK, NY 10012
USA
617-216-1814
AYA@AYAIKEGAYA.COM
WWW.AYAIKEGAYA.COM

0390
ART DIRECTOR: Aya Ikegaya
CLIENT: Lindsay Ackroyd

0476
ART DIRECTOR: Aya Ikegaya
CLIENT: Aya Ikegaya

B.L.A. DESIGN COMPANY
521 SOUTH HOLLY ST.
COLUMBIA, S C
29205
USA
803-518-4130
BRANDIE@BLADESIGNCO.COM

0514, 0516
ART DIRECTOR: Brandi Larisey
Avant
DESIGNER: Brandi Larisey Avant
CLIENT: Self

BANDITO DESIGN CO.
57 SMITH PLACE, APT. 2
COLUMBUS, OH 43201
USA
419-566-1849
RBRINKERHOFF.1@GMAIL.COM
WWW.BANDITODESIGNCO.COM

0220, 0402, 0612, 0678, 0681
DESIGNER: Ryan Brinkerhoff
CLIENT: Self

0667
DESIGNER: Ryan Brinkerhoff
CLIENT: The Chairs
(www.thechairsband.com)

BARBIERI & GREEN
1926 N ST., NW, SECOND FLOOR
WASHINGTON, DC 20036
USA
202-857-0567
JOSH@BGDC.NET
WWW.BGDC.NET

0879
ART DIRECTOR: Adriana Barbieri
DESIGNER: AdrianaBarbieri
CLIENT: American Hospital
Association

BARNHART
1732 CHAMPA ST.
DENVER, CO 80205
USA
303-626-7200
JHARGREAVES@BARNHARTUSA.
COM
WWW.BARNHARTUSA.COM

0562, 0564, 0576
ART DIRECTOR: Joel Hill, Danen
Brickel
DESIGNER: Jim Hargreaves
CLIENT: Barnhart

0944
DESIGNER: Tasso Stathopulos,
Jim Hargreaves

BBMG
200 PARK AVE. S., SUITE 1516
NEW YORK, NY 10003
USA
212-473-4902
SKETCHUM@BBMG.COM
WWW.BBMG.COM

0914
ART DIRECTOR: Scott Ketchum
DESIGNER: Scott Ketchum
CLIENT: BBMG

BEERINBLIK.BE
DICHTERSSTRAAT 85
2610 WILRYK, ANTWERP
BELGIUM
32 486 10 66 14
TOM.MANNAERTS@TELENET.BE
WWW.BEERINBLIK.BE

0629
ART DIRECTOR: Tom Mannaerts
DESIGNER: Tom Mannaerts

BENWILSONART.COM
5716 N. MARCLIFFE AVE.
BOISE, ID 83704
USA
208-869-7982
BENWILSO@GMAIL.COM
WWW.BENWILSONART.COM

0685
ART DIRECTOR: Ben Wilson
DESIGNER: Ben Wilson
CLIENT: The Record Exchange

0686 – 0688
ART DIRECTOR: Ben Wilson
DESIGNER: Ben Wilson
CLIENT: The Crystal Ballroom

BERGWORKS GBM
241 ELDRIDGE ST., 3R
NEW YORK, NY 10002
USA
212-254-6542
LG@BERGWORKS.COM
WWW.BERGWORKS.COM

0998
ART DIRECTOR: Lou Greenberg
DESIGNER: Lou Greenberg
CLIENT: Municipal Art Society

BLANCA GÓMEZ/COSAS MINIMAS
C/MOREJÓN.8
3-R, 28010 MAJOR D
SPAIN
(34) 696 102096
INFO@COSASMINIMAS.COM
WWW.COSASMINIMAS

0001, 0002, 0095, 0797
ART DIRECTOR: Blanca Gómez/
Cosas Minimas
DESIGNER: Blanca Gómez/Cosas
Minimas
CLIENT: Personal

BOB DINETZ DESIGN
210 POST ST., #404
SAN FRANCISCO, CA 94108
USA
415-391-0667
HELLO@BOBDINETZDESIGN.COM
WWW.BOBDINETZDESIGN.COM

0658
ART DIRECTOR: Bob Dinetz
DESIGNER: Bob Dinetz
CLIENT: SFMOMA/ Mika Tajima

BOB'S YOUR UNCLE
25 CHANNEL CENTER ST., #101
BOSTON, MA 02210
USA
617-670-3782
MARTIN@BOBSYOURUNCLECOM
WWW.BOBSYOURUNCLE.COM

0031, 0033, 0035, 0037,
0039 – 0057
DESIGNER: Martin Yeeles
CLIENT: Bob's Your Uncle

BRIAN BEDNARSKI
53 HANCOCK ST.
SOMERVILLE, MA 02144
USA
201-575-0554
BRIANBEDNARSKI@GMAIL.COM
WWW.BRIANBEDNARSKI.COM

0853
ART DIRECTOR: Carrie Jones
DESIGNER: Brian Bednarski
CLIENT: Self

**BRIAN BEDNARSKI,
CARRIE JONES**
53 HANCOCK ST.
SOMERVILLE, MA 02144
USA
201-575-0554
BRIANBEDNARSKI@GMAIL.COM
WWW.BRIANBEDNARSKI.COM

0790
ART DIRECTOR: Carrie Jones
DESIGNER: Brian Bednarski
CLIENT: Ourselves

**BRIAN KROEKER DESIGN FOR
ART & INDUSTRY**
98 EDWIN AVE.
TORONTO
CANADA
416-702-3324
HELLO@BRIANKROEKER.COM
WWW.BRIANKROEKER.COM

0614
DESIGNER: Brian Kroeker
CLIENT: Consultec

BRODY BOYER
148 NELSON ST., APT. 2
BROOKLYN, NY 11231
USA
646-643-9761
BRODYBOYER@HOTMAIL.COM

0816
DESIGNER: Brody Boyer
CLIENT: Lola Conde & Adam
Danforth

BRONSON MA CREATIVE
17700 COPPER SUNSET
SAN ANTONIO, TX 78232
USA
214-457-5615
INFO@BRONSONMA.COM
WWW.BRONSONMA.COM

0559
DESIGNER: Bronson Ma
CLIENT: Bronson Ma Creative

BROWN SUGAR DESIGN
22524 49 AVE., SE
BOTHELL, WA 98021
USA
425-830-3680
INFO@BSDSTUDIO.COM
WWW.BSDSTUDIO.COM

0840
DESIGNER: Jonathan & Whitney
Speir
CLIENT: Elena Martin

0920
DESIGNER: Jonathan & Whitney
Speir
CLIENT: Brown Sugar Design and
Woodland Flowers

BUREAU OF INVITATIONS
400 N. CHURCH ST.,
SUITE 615
CHARLOTTE, NORTH CAROLINA
28202
USA
704-564-8900
ONFO@BUREAUOFINVITATIONS.COM
WWW.BUREAUOFINVITATIONS.COM

0776
ART DIRECTOR: Lauren Felton-
Boynton, David Eller
DESIGNER: David Eller
CLIENT: Andrew Boynton and
Lauren Felton

BURO-LAMP, AMSTERDAM
BORNEOSTRAAT 64H
1094 CM, AMSTERDAM
NETHERLANDS
(+31)20-4707607
MAARTEN@BURO-LAMP.NL
WWW.BURO-LAMP.NL

0547
ART DIRECTOR: Nynke Landman
DESIGNER: Maarten Janssens
CLIENT: buro-Lamp/private

**C3 – CREATIVE CONSUMER
CONCEPTS**
10955 GRANADA LANE
OVERLAND PARK, KS 66211
USA
913-491-6444
CEVANS@C3MAIL.COM
WWW.C3BRANDMARKETING.COM

0952
EXECUTIVE CREATIVE DIRECTOR:
Chris Evans
SR. ILLUSTRATOR/DESIGNER: Matt
Hawkins
SR. COPYWRITER: Ashley Bowles

0955
DESIGNER: Michelle Rader
EXECUTIVE CREATIVE DIRECTOR:
Chris Evans
ASSOCIATE ART DIRECTOR:
Ed Schlittenhardt
SR. COPYWRITER: Ashley Bowles

CABIN + CUB DESIGN
201-55 E. 10TH AVE.
VANCOUVER, BC, V5T 1Y9
CANADA
778-840-7696
VALERIE@CABINANDCUB.COM
WWW.CABINANDCUB.COM;
WWW.CABIN.ETSY.COM

0532
ART DIRECTOR: Valerie Thai
DESIGNER: Valerie Thai

CACAO DESIGN
CORSO SAN GOTTARDO 18
20136 MILANO
ITALY
39 02 89422896
MAURO@CACAODESIGN.IT
WWW.CACAODESIGN.IT

0454
ART DIRECTOR: Creative Staff
DESIGNER: Alessandro Floridia
CLIENT: www.fontegrafica.it

0536
ART DIRECTOR: Creative Staff
DESIGNER: Laura Mangano
CLIENT: lorenzoscaccini.com

0546
ART DIRECTOR: Creative Staff
DESIGNER: Giulia Landini
CLIENT: Tribu Food Design

0798
ART DIRECTOR: Creative Staff
DESIGNER: Giulia Landini
CLIENT: Luca E Sabrina

0856
ART DIRECTOR: Creative Staff
DESIGNER: Laura Mangano
CLIENT: Luxottica

0857
ART DIRECTOR: Creative Staff
DESIGNER: Paola Veronesi
CLIENT: www.lepinete.it

0951
ART DIRECTOR: Creative Staff
DESIGNER: Alessandro Floridia
CLIENT: Vittorio e Federica

0992
ART DIRECTOR: Creative Staff
DESIGNER: Alessandro Floridia
CLIENT: www.fontegrafica.it

CARMEDIA DESIGN
237 S. TERRACE DR.
WICHITA, KS 67218
USA
316-210-9084
INFO@CARMEDIADESIGN.COM
WWW.CARMEDIADESIGN.COM

0838
ART DIRECTOR: Melissa Carduff
DESIGNER: Melissa Carduff
CLIENT: Brian & Melissa Carduff

0888
ART DIRECTOR: Melissa Carduff
DESIGNER: Melissa Carduff
CLIENT: Sherwood Construction

CAROL MCLEOD DESIGN
766 FALMOUTH RD., D-18
MASHPEE, MA 02649
USA
508-477-7482
CAROL@CAROLMCLEODDESIGN.COM
WWW.CAROLMCLEODDESIGN.COM

0405
ART DIRECTOR: Carol McLeod
DESIGNER: Chris Daigneault, Amy
Caracappa-Obeck
CLIENT: Carol McLeod Design

**CASSIE HESTER DESIGN +
ILLUSTRATION**
1231 CASTLE DR.
WATKINSVILLE, GA 30677
USA
766-296-6712
CASSIEHESTER@GMAIL.COM
WWW.CASSIEHESTER.COM

0386
DESIGNER: Cassie Hester

0613
DESIGNER: Cassie Hester
CLIENT: Local Teen/Tween Book
Club

CAUSE DESIGN CO.
379 W. GLENSIDE AVE.
GLENSIDE, PA 19038
USA
215-886-0697
RODD@CAUSEDESIGN.COM
WWW.CAUSEDESIGN.COM

0555
ART DIRECTOR: Rodd Whitney
DESIGNER: Rodd Whitney
CLIENT: Keith Humphreys Realtor

0632
ART DIRECTOR: Rodd Whitney
DESIGNER: Rodd Whitney
CLIENT:Jerry + Hesed Fourroux

0924
ART DIRECTOR: Rodd Whitney
DESIGNER: Rodd Whitney
CLIENT: University of Arizona,
Eller School of Management

CDRYAN
6 TAYLOR ST.
PORTLAND, ME 04102
USA
347-403-2781
CDRYAN@CDRYAN.COM
WWW.CDRYAN.COM

0637 – 0640
ART DIRECTOR: Christopher David
Ryan
DESIGNER: Christopher David Ryan

**CHRIS ROONEY ILLUSTRATION/
DESIGN**
1317 SANTA FE AVE.
BERKELEY, CA 94702
USA
415-827-3729
CHRIS@LOONEYROONEY.COM
WWW.LOONEYROONEY.COM

0406, 0502, 0511
ART DIRECTOR: Chris Rooney
DESIGNER: Chris Rooney

0628
ART DIRECTOR: Chris Rooney
DESIGNER: Chris Rooney
CLIENT: Avery Bruen

0633
ART DIRECTOR: Chris Rooney
DESIGNER: Chris Rooney
CLIENT: Beck Martin Rooney

CHRIS TRIVIZAS I DESIGN
161 SYGROU AVE., NEA SMIRNI
ATHENS, ATTIKI 171 21
GREECE
CONTACT@CHRISTRIVIZAS.GR
WWW.CHRISTRIVIZAS.GR

0550
ART DIRECTOR: Chris Trivizas
DESIGNER: Chris Trivizas
CLIENT: Chris Trivizas

0551
ART DIRECTOR: Chris Trivizas
DESIGNER: Chris Trivizas
CLIENT: Kostas & Maria Kontou

**CLAUDIA PEARSON
ILLUSTRATION**
141 GREEN AVE., #2
BROOKLYN, NY 11238
USA
718-789-9507
CLAUDIAPEARSON@GMAIL.COM
WWW.CLAUDIAPEARSON.COM

0060, 0091, 0097, 0099, 0239

CLEAR MARKETING
121 PALATINE RD.
DIDSBURY, MANCHESTER
UK
0161 448 8008
JAMESGREENAWAY@
CLEARMARKETING.CO.UK
WWW.CLEARMARKETING.CO.UK

0499
ART DIRECTOR:James Greenaway
DESIGNER: James Greenaway
CLIENT: David Birtwistle

COOPER GRAPHIC DESIGN
50 WESTVIEW ST.
PHILADELPHIA, PA 19119
USA
215-844-1661
MICHELE@
COOPERGRAPHICDESIGN.COM
WWW.COOPERGRAPHICDESIGN.COM

0605
ART DIRECTOR: Gavin Cooper
DESIGNER: Gavin Cooper, John
Burns
CLIENT: AIGA Philadelphia

COPIA CREATIVE, INC.
3122 SANTA MONICA BLVD.,
SUITE 203
SANTA MONICA, CA 90404
USA
310-826-7422
MICHELLE@COPIACREATIVE.COM
WWW.COPIACREATIVE.COM

0553, 0563
CLIENT: YPO

0566, 0587
CLIENT: Self

CORAL & TUSK
426 STERLING PLACE, APT. #1A
BROOKLYN, NY 11238
USA
917-586-3582
STEPHANIE@CORALANDTUSK.COM
WWW.CORALANDTUSK.COM

0131 – 0133, 0136
ART DIRECTOR: Stephanie Housley
DESIGNER: Stephanie Housley

COULSON MACLEOD
49 CARLTON ST.
KETTERING NN16 8ED
UK
01536 482771
ENQUIRIES@COULSONMACLEOD.COM
WWW.COULSONMACLEOD.COM

0645 – 0648
ART DIRECTOR: Mark Coulson
DESIGNER: Mark Coulson

CRACKED DESIGNS LLC
359 E. MONTANA
MILWAUKEE, WI 53207
USA
414-687-8803
TARASHERM@GMAIL.COM
WWW.CRACKED-DESIGNS.COM

0026, 0197
DESIGNER: Tara Scheuerman

CRANKY PRESSMAN
150 PENN AVE.
SALEM, OR 44460
USA
800-433-1288
JAMIE@CRANKYPRESSMAN.COM
WWW.CRANKYPRESSMAN.COM;
WWW.ER-H.COM

0507
ART DIRECTOR: Jamie Berger
CLIENT: Self
ILLUSTRATOR: Eric Hanson

0584
ART DIRECTOR: Jamie Berger
CLIENT: Self
ILLUSTRATOR: Dave Flaherty

0586
ART DIRECTOR: Jamie Berger
DESIGNER: Mickey Burton
CLIENT: Self

CREATIVE SQUALL
507 INDIAN CREEK DR.
TROPHY CLUB, TX 76262
USA
214-244-5011
TAD@CREATIVESQUALL.COM
WWW.CREATIVESQUALL.COM

0778
ART DIRECTOR: Tad Dobbs
DESIGNER: Tad Dobbs
CLIENT: Blair Highfill

CROWDED TEETH
1229 N. EL MOLINO AVE.
PASADENA, CA 91104
USA
818-458-6558
MICHELLE@CROWDEDTEETH.COM
WWW.CROWDEDTEETH.COM

0280 – 0298
ART DIRECTOR: Michelle Romo
DESIGNER: Michelle Romo
CLIENT: Creatives Inc.

CURIOUS GRAVY
1000 S. CATALINA AVE.
REDONDO BEACH, CA
USA
310-415-4965
CURIOUSGRAVY@ME.COM
WWW.CURIOUSGRAVY.COM

0137

CUTIEPIE COMPANY
USA
917-549-0627
MILLYITZHAK@YAHOO.COM
WWW.CUTIEPIECOMPANY.COM;
WWW.CUTIEPIECOMPANY.ETSY.COM

0222, 0459
ART DIRECTOR: Milly Itzhak

DAIS
SUITE 10, 36 AGNES ST.
FORTITUDE VALLEY QLD 4006
AUSTRALIA
BETH@DAIS.COM.AU
WWW.DAIS.COM.AU

0549
ART DIRECTOR: Travers Murr
DESIGNER: Steve Younger
CLIENT: Dais

DANIELLE ZENK, CHAD TILLS
4215 BLAISDELL AVE. S.
MINNEAPOLIS, MN 55409
USA
612-799-3577
DANIELLE.ZENK@GMAIL.COM

0785
ART DIRECTOR: Danielle Zenk,
Chad Tills
DESIGNER: Danielle Zenk, Chad Tills
CLIENT: Danielle Zenk, Chad Tills

DARLING CLEMENTINE
URAWIENBORG TERRASSE, NO. 9
0351 OSLO
NORWAY
0047 47275182
POST@DARLINGCLEMENTINE.NO
WWW.DARLINGCLEMENTINE.NO

0110 – 0115, 0118 – 0129
ART DIRECTOR: Darling Clementine
DESIGNER: Darling Clementine
CLIENT: Darling Clementine

DAVID CLARK DESIGN
1305 E. 15TH, SUITE 202
TULSA, OK 74120
USA
918-295-0044
INFO@DAVIDCLARKDESIGN.COM
WWW.DAVIDCLARKDESIGN.COM

0442
ART DIRECTOR: David Clark
DESIGNER: Nate Olsen, Becky
Gelder, David Clark
CLIENT: David Clark Design

0462, 0513
ART DIRECTOR: David Clark
DESIGNER: Becky Gelder, David
Clark
CLIENT: David Clark Design

0956
ART DIRECTOR: David Clark
DESIGNER: Nate Olsen,
David Clark
CLIENT: Dentsply Tulsa Dental
Specialties

DAVID SENIOR
8 DOE DR.
BLACKWOOD, NJ 08012
USA
215-740-9370
DAVE@DAVIDSENIORILLUSTRATION.COM
WWW.DAVIDSENIORILLUSTRATION.COM

0434
ART DIRECTOR: David Senior
DESIGNER: David Senior
CLIENT: David Senior

0835
ART DIRECTOR: David Senior
CLIENT: Annie Harder + Evan
Gordley

0836
DESIGNER: David Senior, Colin
McSherry
CLIENT: Cassandra Jenkins

DAVIES ASSOCIATES
9424 DAYTON WAY, SUITE 217
BEVERLY HILLS, CA 90210
USA
310-247-9572
CDAVIES@DAVIESLA.COM
WWW.DAVIESLA.COM

0490
ART DIRECTOR: Cathy Davies
DESIGNER: Paul Hershfield
CLIENT: Davies Associates

DEAN JAMES BALLAS
2738 W. GREENLEAF ST.
ALLENTOWN, PA 18104
USA
610-739-6878
DEANBALLAS@YAHOO.COM
COROFLOT.COM/DEANBALLAS

0959
ART DIRECTOR: Dean James
Ballas
DESIGNER: Dean James Ballas
CLIENT: Charles T. Crawford

DESIGN DES TROY
320 ELSIE ST.
SAN FRANCISCO, CA 94110
USA
415-706-5210
DESIGN@DES-TROY.COM
HTTP://DESIGN.DES-TROY.COM

**0011, 0058, 0063, 0204, 0359,
0407**
ART DIRECTOR: Samantha Troy,
Owen Troy

0825
ART DIRECTOR: Samantha Troy,
Owen Troy
CLIENT: Michelle Lutsky + Hal
Lutsky

DESIGNTACTICS
UNIT E7, NUTGROVE OFFICE PARK
NUTGROVE AVE, DUBLIN 14
IRELAND
353 1 207 9107
BRENDAN@DESIGNTACTICS.NET
WWW.DESIGNTACTICS.NET

0528
ART DIRECTOR: Brendan Donlon
DESIGNER: Jonny Murphy
CLIENT: Designtactics

DKNG STUDIOS
1531 HARVARD ST.
SANTA MONICA, CA 90404
USA
310-910-1599
CONTACT@DKNGSTUDIOS.COM
WWW.DKNGSTUDIOS.COM

0690
ART DIRECTOR: Dan Kuhlken,
Nathan Goldman
DESIGNER: Dan Kuhlken, Nathan
Goldman
CLIENT: The Hotel Cafe Tour

0700
ART DIRECTOR: Dan Kuhlken,
Nathan Goldman
DESIGNER: Dan Kuhlken, Nathan
Goldman
CLIENT: The Swell Season (bear)

0701
ART DIRECTOR: Dan Kuhlken,
Nathan Goldman
DESIGNER: Dan Kuhlken, Nathan
Goldman
CLIENT: Firs

0702
ART DIRECTOR: Dan Kuhlken,
Nathan Goldman
DESIGNER: Dan Kuhlken, Nathan
Goldman
CLIENT: Iron & Wine

0703
ART DIRECTOR: Dan Kuhlken,
Nathan Goldman
DESIGNER: Dan Kuhlken, Nathan
Goldman
CLIENT: The Swell Season (deer)

0704
ART DIRECTOR: Dan Kuhlken,
Nathan Goldman
DESIGNER: Dan Kuhlken, Nathan
Goldman
CLIENT: Monsters of Folk

0706
ART DIRECTOR: Dan Kuhlken,
Nathan Goldman
DESIGNER: Dan Kuhlken, Nathan
Goldman
CLIENT: AC Newman

0707
ART DIRECTOR: Dan Kuhlken,
Nathan Goldman
DESIGNER: Dan Kuhlken, Nathan
Goldman
CLIENT: Kina Grannis

0712
ART DIRECTOR: Dan Kuhlken,
Nathan Goldman
DESIGNER: Dan Kuhlken, Nathan
Goldman
CLIENT: It's Always Sunny in
Philadelphia

0727
ART DIRECTOR: Dan Kuhlken,
Nathan Goldman
DESIGNER: Dan Kuhlken, Nathan
Goldman
CLIENT: Flight of the Conchords

DONNA KARAN IN-HOUSE
240 W. 40TH ST.
NEW YORK, NY 10018
USA
212-768-6196
AIKEGAYA@DKINTL.COM
WWW.DKNY.COM

0479, 0904
ART DIRECTOR: Paul Tedesco
DESIGNER: Aya Ikegaya
CLIENT: DKNY

0900
ART DIRECTOR: Paul Tedesco
DESIGNER: Grace Chu
CLIENT: Donna Karan Intl.

0902
ART DIRECTOR: Paul Tedesco
DESIGNER: Aya Ikegaya
CLIENT: Donna Karan

DOUBLENAUT
CANADA

0276 – 0279
ART DIRECTOR: Matt McCracken
DESIGNER: Matt McCracken

0697
ART DIRECTOR: Matt Mccracken
DESIGNER: Matt Mccracken
CLIENT: Mogwai

0698
ART DIRECTOR: Matt McCracken
DESIGNER: Matt McCracken
CLIENT: Monsters of Folk

0699
ART DIRECTOR: Andrew McCracken
DESIGNER: Andrew McCracken
CLIENT: The Swell Season /
Overcoat Management

0708
ART DIRECTOR: Matt McCracken
DESIGNER: McCracken
CLIENT: Myspace Canada

0709
ART DIRECTOR: Matt McCracken
DESIGNER: Matt McCracken
CLIENT: Future of the Left

DOUG CLOUSE
150 W. 95TH ST., 7D
NEW YORK, NY 10025
USA
646-423-0501
DCLOUSE@MAC.COM

0649, 0679
ART DIRECTOR:
DESIGNER: Angela Voulangas,
Doug Clouse
CLIENT: Angela Voulangas, Doug
Clouse

DRAGON ROUGE
54 W. 21ST ST., SUITE 905
NEW YORK, NY 10010
USA
212-367-8800
BRODY@DRAGONROUGE-USA.COM
WWW.DRAGONROUGE-USA.COM

0435, 0491
ART DIRECTOR: Marcus Dewitt
DESIGNER: Brody Boyer
CLIENT: Dragon Rouge

DUDE AND CHICK
PO BOX 4292
ST. PAUL. MN 55104
USA
651-674-7917
CHICK@DUDEANDCHICK.COM
WWW.DUDEANDCHICK.COM

0199, 0219, 0224, 0225
DESIGNER: Katie Wilson, John
Gurtin

EGE SOYUER
85 BLACKBERRY DR.
STAMFORD, CT 06903
USA
914-584-9840
ESOYUER@GMAIL.COM
WWW.EGESOYUER.COM

0651, 0652
ART DIRECTOR: Ege Soyuer
DESIGNER: Ege Soyuer
CLIENT: Purchase College School
of Art + Design

ELEMENTS
20 GRAND AVE.
NEW HAVEN, CT 06513
USA
203-776-1323
STUDIO@ELEMENTSDESIGN.COM
WWW.ELEMENTSDESIGN.COM;
WWW.HELLOELEMENTS.COM

0430
ART DIRECTOR: Amy Graver
DESIGNER: Kerry Ober
CLIENT: Elements

0626
ART DIRECTOR: Amy Graver
DESIGNER: Amy Graver
CLIENT: Amy & Scott Graver

ELEVATED PRESS
106 DEPOT ST.
ANN ARBOR, MI 48104
USA
734-786-8460
INFO@ELEVATEDPRESS.COM
WWW.ELEVATEDPRESS.COM

**0092 – 0094, 0096, 0100, 0501,
0821, 0849, 0850**
ART DIRECTOR: Michelle Baker
DESIGNER: Michelle Baker

ELEVEN1111ELEVEN DESIGN
SUITE 141, 30 FOVEAUX ST.
SURRY HILLS, NSW, 2010
AUSTRALIA
SHELLEY@ELEVENELEVEN.COM.AU
WWW.ELEVENELEVEN.COM.AU

0578
ART DIRECTOR: Lindsay Smith
DESIGNER: Lindsay Smith
CLIENT: Eleven1111Eleven Design

EMILIA LÓPEZ
MAGDALENENSTR. 21125
1065 VIENA
AUSTRIA
CONTACT@EMILIALOPEZ.COM
WWW.EMILIALOPEZ.COM

0466
ART DIRECTOR: Emilia López
DESIGNER: Emilia López
CLIENT: Self

EMILY ANN DESIGNS
9230 PHINNEY AVE. N.
SEATTLE, WA 98103
USA
425-772-5901
EMILYANNTRVONG@HOTMAIL.COM
WWW.EMILYANNDESIGNS.ETSY.COM

0233 – 0235, 0354
ART DIRECTOR: Emily Trvong
DESIGNER: Emily Trvong

EMORY CASH DESIGN
409 LEGRAND BLVD.
GREENVILLE, SC 29607
USA
864-982-4309
EMORY.CASH@GMAIL.COM
WWW.EMORYCASH.COM

0696
ART DIRECTOR: Emory Cash
DESIGNER: Emory Cash
CLIENT: Spartanburg Little Theatre

0808
ART DIRECTOR: Emory Cash
DESIGNER: Emory Cash
CLIENT: Keri Burger + Carter
Tippins

EP DESIGNWORKS
1017 CATHEDRAL DR.
SUFFOLK, VA 23434
USA
757-619-3244
GRAPHICS@EPDESIGNWORKS.COM
WWW.EPDESIGNWORKS.COM

0540 – 0542
ART DIRECTOR: Eugene Phillips
DESIGNER: Eugene Phillips
CLIENT: EP Designworks

ERIN BAZOS
120 NORTH 7TH ST., #4B
BROOKLYN, NY 11211
USA
646-327-6585
ERIN@ERINBAZOS.COM
WWW.ERINBAZOS.COM

0800
DESIGNER: Erin Bazos
CLIENT: Erin & Erich

0847
DESIGNER: Erin Bazos
CLIENT: Adrienne & Willson

EVA JANE HOGAN
7 CAMBRIDGE TCE.
RANELACH, DUBLIN 6
IRELAND
353 86 1567 444
EVAJANEHOGAN@GMAIL.COM
WWW.EVAJANEHOGAN.COM

0634
ART DIRECTOR: Eva Jane Hogan
DESIGNER: Eva Jane Hogan

EXPLORARE
CHINANTLA #9. COL. LA PAZ
PUEBLA, PUE. 72160
MEXICO
52 (222) 230-4152
INFO@EXPLORARE.COM
WWW.EXPLORARE.COM

0889
DESIGNER: Juan Carlos Henaine
CLIENT: Blas Cernicchiaro Maimone

FINISHED ART INC.
708 ANTONE ST.
ATLANTA, GA 30318
USA
404-355-7902
KIM@FINISHEDART.COM
WWW.FINISHEDART.COM

0450
ART DIRECTOR: Li Kim Goh
DESIGNER: Li Kim Goh & Mj Hasek
CLIENT: Self

FOREIGN POLICY DESIGN GROUP
231A SOUTH BRIDGE RD.
SINGAPORE 058780
SINGAPORE
65 6222 0878
AFFAIRS@FOREIGNPOLICYLTD.COM
WWW.FOREIGNPOLICYDESIGN.COM

0594 – 0596
ART DIRECTOR: Yah-Leng Yu
DESIGNER: Yah-Leng Yu, Tianyu
Isaiah Zheng
CLIENT: Self

FOSSIL
8600 SPECTRUM DR.
MCKINNEY, TX 75070
USA
469-742-0080
CASEY@INKYLIPSPRESS.COM
WWW.INKYLIPSPRESS.COM

0680
DESIGNER: Tim Hale
CLIENT: Fossil

FOUNDRY
1425 9 AVE. SE
CALGARY, AB T2G 0T4
CANADA
403-237-8044
ZAHRA@FOUNDRYCREATIVE.CA
WWW.FOUNDRYCREATIVE.CA

0630
ART DIRECTOR: Zahra Al-Havazi
DESIGNER: Zahra Al-Havazi
CLIENT: Kylie Henry

0939
ART DIRECTOR: Zahra Al-Harazi
DESIGNER: Louise Uhrenholt
CLIENT: Banff Park Lodge

GAGATREE PTE LTD
237 ALEXANDRA RD. #04-12
THE ALEXCIER, SINGAPORE
159929
SINGAPORE
65 62960170
TRACY@GAGATREE.COM
WWW.GAGATREE.COM

0464
ART DIRECTOR: Yang Qiao'E
DESIGNER: Yang Qiao'e
CLIENT: Gagatree Pte Ltd

0486
ART DIRECTOR: Yang Qiao'E
DESIGNER: Lester Lim
CLIENT: Gagatree Pte Ltd

0487
ART DIRECTOR: Yang Qiao'E
DESIGNER: Stop Lee
CLIENT: Gagatree Pte Ltd

0488
ART DIRECTOR: Yang Qiao'E
DESIGNER: Sam Har
CLIENT: Gagatree Pte Ltd

**GARY HOUSTON DESIGN /
VOODOO CATBOX**
6700 N. NEW YORK AVE., SUITE 211
PORTLAND, OR 97203
USA
503-248-0510
GARY@VOODOOCATBOX.COM
WWW.VOODOOCATBOX.COM

0774
ART DIRECTOR: Gary Houston
DESIGNER: Gary Houston
CLIENT: Los Lobos

0775
ART DIRECTOR: Gary Houston
DESIGNER: Gary Houston
CLIENT: The Dead

GEE + CHUNG DESIGN
38 BRYANT STREET, SUITE 100
SAN FRANCISCO, CA 94105
USA
415-543-1192
EARL@GEECHUNGDESIGN.COM
WWW.GEECHUNGDESIGN.COM

0676, 0935, 0936, 0950, 0954
ART DIRECTOR: Earl Gee
DESIGNER: Earl Gee, Fani Chung
CLIENT: DCM

GERARD DESIGN
28371 DAVIS PARKWAY, SUITE 100
WARRENVILLE, IL 60555
USA
630-355-0775
KAM@GERARDDESIGN.COM

0942
ART DIRECTOR: Patrick Schab
DESIGNER: Patrick Schab
CLIENT: Self

GEYRHALTER DESIGN
2525 MAIN ST., SUITE 205
SANTA MONICA, CA 90405
USA
310-392-7615
FABIAN@GEYRHALTER.COM
WWW.GEYRHALTER.COM

0447
ART DIRECTOR: Fabian Geyrhalter
DESIGNER: Julia Hou
CLIENT: Geyrhalter Design

GIANESINI DESIGN
1123 BROADWAY, SUITE 305
NEW YORK, NY 10010
USA
212-807-0634
MAIL@GIANESINIDESIGN.COM
WWW.GIANESINIDESIGN.COM

0412, 0413
ART DIRECTOR: Tina Gianesini
DESIGNER: Tina Gianesini
CLIENT: MR Architecture

GILAH PRESS + DESIGN
3506 ASH ST.
BALTIMORE, MD 21211
USA
410-746-9059
INFO@GILAHPRESS.COM
WWW.GILAHPRESS.COM

0357
ART DIRECTOR: Kat Feuerstein
DESIGNER: Anup Pradhan
CLIENT: Gilah Press + Design

0384
ART DIRECTOR: Kat Feuerstein
DESIGNER: Nathalie Wilson
CLIENT: Gilah Press + Design

0395, 0919
ART DIRECTOR: Kat Feuerstein
DESIGNER: Kat Feuerstein
CLIENT: Gilah Press + Design

0400
ART DIRECTOR: Kat Feuerstein
DESIGNER: Whitney Cecil
CLIENT: Gilah Press + Design

0449
ART DIRECTOR: Kat Feuerstein
DESIGNER: Luke Williams
CLIENT: Gilah Press + Design

0533
ART DIRECTOR: Kat Feuerstein
DESIGNER: Alison Medland
CLIENT: Gilah Press + Design

GRAVES FOWLER CREATIVE
5515 SECURITY LANE, SUITE 1109
ROCKVILLE, MD 20852
USA
301-816-0097 X305
MARIANN@GRAVESFOWLER.COM
WWW.GRAVESFOWLER.COM

0601
ART DIRECTOR: Mariann Seriff
DESIGNER: Victoria Q. Robinson,
Jeffrey Everett, Mariann Seriff
CLIENT: Self

GREENLIGHT DESIGNS
11206 WEDDINGTON ST., 2ND
FLOOR
N. HOLLYWOOD, CA 91601
USA
818-509-0787
MELISSA@GREENLIGHTDESIGNS.NET
WWW.GREENLIGHTDESIGNS.NET

0870, 0871, 0962
ART DIRECTOR: Melissa Irwin
DESIGNER: Shaun Wood
CLIENT: Teena Hostovich
CREATIVE DIRECTOR: Tami Shelly
ACCOUNT EXECUTIVE: Darryl Shelly
PROJECT MANAGER: Luz Mendoza

0964
ART DIRECTOR: Melissa Irwin
DESIGNER: Shaun Wood
CLIENT: Shizué
CREATIVE DIRECTOR: Tami Shelly
ACCOUNT EXECUTIVE: Darryl Shelly
PROJECT MANAGER: Luz Mendoza

0972
ART DIRECTOR: Melissa Irwin
DESIGNER: Shaun Wood
CLIENT: Greenlight Designs
CREATIVE DIRECTOR: Tami Shelly
ACCOUNT EXECUTIVE: Darryl Shelly
PROJECT MANAGER: Luz Mendoza

GREENWICH LETTERPRESS
39 CHRISTOPHER ST.
NEW YORK, NY 10014
USA
212-989-7464
INFO@GREENWICHLETTERPRESS.COM
WWW.GREENWICHLETTERPRESS.COM

**0223, 0355, 0356, 0358, 0498,
0823, 0833, 0837**
DESIGNER: Amy Swanson

GREGORY BEAUCHAMP
42 NAVY ST., #4
VENICE, CA 90291
USA
310-922-5481
GREG@BEAUCHAMPING.COM
WWW.BEAUCHAMPING.COM

0641 – 0644
CLIENT: Self

GRETEMAN GROUP
1425 E. DOUGLAS, FLOOR 2
WICHITA, KS 67211
USA
316-263-1004
CFARROW@GRETEMANGROUP.COM
WWW.GRETEMANGROUP.COM

0428
ART DIRECTOR: Sonia Greteman
DESIGNER: Chris Parks
CLIENT: Bombardier Learjet

0444, 0445
ART DIRECTOR: Sonia Greteman
DESIGNER: Garrett Fresh
CLIENT: Bombardier Flexjet

0927
ART DIRECTOR: Sonia Greteman
DESIGNER: Garrett Fresh
CLIENT: Signature Flight Support

0931
ART DIRECTOR: Sonia Greteman
DESIGNER: Craig Tomson
CLIENT: Lawkingdon Architecture

**GROSSET & DUNLAP
(AN IMPRINT OF PENGUIN
PUBLISHERS)**
345 HUDSON ST., FLOOR 14
NEW YORK NY 10014
USA
212-414-3624
MEAGAN.BENNETT@
US.PENGUINGROUP.COM
WWW.US.PENGUINGROUP.COM/
YOUNGREADERS

0458
ART DIRECTOR: Adam Royce
DESIGNER: Meagan Bennett
CLIENT: In-House

GUTIÉRREZ DESIGN ASSOCIATES
306 MULHOLLAND ST.
ANN ARBOR, MI 48103
USA
734-662-4878
J_GUTIERREZ10-VENDORS@
YAHOO.COM

0859
ART DIRECTOR:
DESIGNER: Jeannette Gutíerrez
CLIENT: Andrés Blibeche

HA DESIGN
19066 E. MAUNA LOA AVE.
GLENDORA, CA 91740
USA
626-475-6606
HACREATIVE@MAC.COM
WWW.CREATIVEHOTLIST.COM/
H_ATMALI

0433
ART DIRECTOR: Handy Atmali
DESIGNER: Handy Atmali
CLIENT: HA Design

0937
ART DIRECTOR: Handy Atmali
DESIGNER: Handy Atmali
CLIENT: Peter + Dina

HALEY STUDIO
134 LAKEWOOD GARDENS LN.
MADISON, WI 53704
USA
608-239-7003
INFO@HALEYSTUDIO.COM
WWW.HALEYSTUDIO.COM

0571
ART DIRECTOR: Enid Williams
DESIGNER: Enid Williams
CLIENT: Erik Nielsen/Tracy Honn

HARDCUORE
RUA FARO, 41 / 603
JARDIM BOTÂNICO, RIO DE
JANEIRO, RJ 22461-020
BRAZIL
55 21 3298-0787
55 21 9353-1035
BRENO@HARDCUORE.COM
WWW.HARDCUORE.COM

0986
ART DIRECTOR: Breno Pineschi
DESIGNER: Breno Pineschi
CLIENT: Natália & Daniel

HATCH DESIGN
353 BROADWAY ST.
SAN FRANCISCO, CA 94133
USA
415-396-1650
NATE@HATCHSF.COM
WWW.HATCHSF.COM

0474
ART DIRECTOR: Katie Jain, Joel
Templin
DESIGNER: Eszter Clark, Ryan Meis
CLIENT: Hatch Design

0530
ART DIRECTOR: Katie Jain, Joel
Templin
DESIGNER: Eszter Clark
CLIENT: Hatch Design

0531
ART DIRECTOR: Katie Jain, Joel
Templin
DESIGNER: Jeffrey Bucholtz
CLIENT: Hatch Design

0554
ART DIRECTOR: Katie Jain, Joel
Templin
DESIGNER: Eszter Clark, Joel
Templin
CLIENT: Hatch Design

0565
ART DIRECTOR: Katie Jain, Joel
Templin
DESIGNER: Katie Jain, Joel
Templin, Ryan Meis, Eszter Clark
CLIENT: JAQK Cellars

HEARTS & ANCHORS
SAN FRANCISCO, CA
USA
415-860-1759
SARAH@HEARTSANDANCHORS.COM
WWW.HEARTSANDANCHORS.COM

0168, 0170
ART DIRECTOR: Sarah L. M. Adler
DESIGNER: Sarah L. M. Adler

0841
ART DIRECTOR: Sarah L. M. Adler
DESIGNER: Sarah L. M. Adler
CLIENT: Melody Houser & Ben
Mahoney

HELEN LAI
61 TOWN CENTRE COURT, UNIT 1901
SCARBOROUGH, ON
CANADA
416-707-8855
HLLH@HOTMAIL.COM

0824, 0845
CLIENT: Self

HELIX
1629 WALNUT ST.
KANSAS CITY MO 64108
USA
816-994-7411
SSANEM@HELIXKC.COM
WWW.HELIXKC.COM

0592
ART DIRECTOR: Shawn Sanem
DESIGNER: Shawn Sanem
CLIENT: Helix

HIJIRIK STUDIO
491 7TH AVE., #2
BROOKLYN, NY 11215
USA
415-205-7400
CONTACT@HIJIRIK.COM
WWW.HIJIRIK.COM

0343 – 0346, 0401, 0403
ART DIRECTOR: Hijiri K. Shepherd
DESIGNER: Hijiri K. Shepherd

HOET & HOET
CHAUSSEE DE LASNE, 42
1330 RIXENSART
BELGIUM
32 2 646 40 06
RONANE.HOET@HOET-HOET.EU
WWW.HOET-HOET.EU

0411
ART DIRECTOR: Hoet & Hoet
DESIGNER: Hoet & Hoet
CLIENT: Hoet & Hoet

HONEST BROS.
1804 S. PEARL ST.
DENVER, CO 80210
USA
303-744-8089 X802
ERIC@HONESTBROS.COM
WWW.HONESTBROS.COM

0543 – 0545
ART DIRECTOR: Eric Hines
DESIGNER: Ryan Lee
CLIENT: Self

HULDRA PRESS
PO BOX 37
PENLAND, NC 28765
USA
215-518-5673
MDAGES@GMAIL.COM
WWW.HULDRAPRESS.COM

**0028, 0382, 0383, 0389,
0392 – 0394**
DESIGNER: Marianne Dages/
Huldra Press

IAN KOENIG
4751 N. VIRGINIA AVE., #1
CHICAGO, IL 60625
USA
617-447-8249
IANKOENIG@MAC.COM
WWW.IANKOENIGPORTFOLIO.COM

0794, 0799
ART DIRECTOR: Ian Koenig
DESIGNER: Ian Koenig

IMAGINE
THE STABLES, DUCIE ST.
MANCHESTER M1 2JN
UK
44 (0) 161 272 8334
INFO@IMAGINE-CGO.CO.UK
WWW.IMAGINE-CGO.CO.UK

0934
ART DIRECTOR: David Caunce
DESIGNER: David Caunce
CLIENT: The Monastery,
Manchester

INKY LIPS LETTERPRESS
8600 SPECTRUM DR.
MCKINNEY, TX 75070
USA
469-742-0080
CASEY@INKYLIPSPRESS.COM
WWW.INKYLIPSPRESS.COM

0525
DESIGNER: Casey Mcgarr
CLIENT: Inky Lips Letterpress

0572, 0866
DESIGNER: Casey Mcgarr
CLIENT: Lindsey

0674
DESIGNER: Casey Mcgarr
CLIENT: High on Fire

0677
DESIGNER: Casey Mcgarr
CLIENT: Phil Hollenbeck

0683
DESIGNER: Virgil Scott, Casey
Mcgarr
CLIENT: The Soda Fallery

0684
DESIGNER: Casey Mcgarr
CLIENT: Clampitt Paper Company

0810
DESIGNER: Casey Mcgarr
CLIENT: Larra & Jarrod

0828
DESIGNER: Casey Mcgarr
CLIENT: Salwa and Dru

0862
DESIGNER: Casey Mcgarr
CLIENT: Guy Rogers

0916
DESIGNER: Casey Mcgarr
CLIENT: Thomas Morris

IRIS A. BROWN DESIGN LLC
106 CABRINI BLVD., SUITE 4D
NEW YORK, NY 10033
USA
212-781-7070
IRIS@IABDNY.COM
WWW.IABDNY.COM

0874
ART DIRECTOR: Iris A. Brown
DESIGNER: Iris A. Brown
CLIENT: 52nd Street Project

0897
ART DIRECTOR: Iris A. Brown
DESIGNER: Iris A. Brown
CLIENT: 92nd Street Y

ISOTOPE 221
232 WASHINGTON AVE., 4TH FLOOR
BROOKLYN, NY 11205
USA
718-783-3092
INFO@ISOTOPE221.COM
WWW.ISOTOPE221.COM

0782
ART DIRECTOR: Christopher Cannon
DESIGNER: Christopher Cannon
CLIENT: Yang Wang &
Christopher Cannon

JAMIE LATENDRESSE DESIGN
28 SICKLES ST., SUITE 17D
NEW YORK, NY 10040
USA
313-657-3579
JAMIE@JAMIELATENDRESSE.COM
WWW.JAMIELATENDRESSE.COM

0269, 0270, 0404
ART DIRECTOR: Jamie Latendresse
DESIGNER: Jamie Latendresse

JANE HANCOCK PAPERS
USA
678-508-5454
RAJSHEL@JHPAPERS.COM
WWW.JHPAPERS.COM

0822
ART DIRECTOR: Rajshel Juhan
CLIENT: Julie Hostettler

0863
ART DIRECTOR: Rajshel Johan
CLIENT: Self
ILLUSTRATOR: Brandon Guterrez

JASON BAILEY
701 PRESIDENT ST.
BROOKLYN, NY 11215
USA
QUINCY.JASON@GMAIL.COM

0657
ART DIRECTOR: Jason Bailey
DESIGNER: Jason Bailey

JOEY'S CORNER
444 DE HARO ST., SUITE 207
SAN FRANCISCO, CA 94107
USA
415-255-0125
SK@MODSF.COM
WWW.JOEYSCORNER.ORG

0880, 0973
ART DIRECTOR: Michael Osborne
DESIGNER: Jeff Ho
CLIENT: Family Services Agency
of San Mateo Hillsborough
Auxiliary

JOHANN A. GÓMEZ
2562 DEXTER AVE. N.
SEATTLE, WASHINGTON 98109
USA
206-999-6643
JAGORAMA@HOTMAIL.COM
WWW.JOHANNGOMEZ.COM

0802
ART DIRECTOR: Johann A. Gómez
DESIGNER: Johann A. Gómez
CLIENT: Jamee R. Smith &
Johann A. Gómez

JONATHAN BARTLETT
77 MONITOR ST., APT. 1F
BROOKLYN, NY 11222
USA
336-345-0369
JB@SEEJBDRAW.COM
WWW.SEEJBDRAW.COM

0577
ART DIRECTOR: Joel Hill, Danen
Brickel
DESIGNER: Jim Hargreaves
CLIENT: Self

JUICEBOX DESIGNS
4709 IDAHO AVE.
NASHVILLE, TN 37209
USA
615-297-1682
INFO@JUICEBOXDESIGNS.COM
WWW.JUICEBOXDESIGNS.COM

0893
ART DIRECTOR: Jay Smith
DESIGNER: Jay Smith
CLIENT: World Vision

JULIA REICH DESIGN
384 MAIN ST., 2ND FLOOR
AURORA, NY 13026
USA
315-364-7190
JULIA@JULIAREICHDESIGN.COM
WWW.JULIAREICHDESIGN.COM

0611
ART DIRECTOR: Julia Reich
DESIGNER: Julia Reich
CLIENT: Self

0926
ART DIRECTOR: Julia Reich
DESIGNER: Julia Reich
CLIENT: Wells College

KAMAI
1915 COLGATE AVE.
RICHMOND, VA 23226
USA
804-814-2911
HELLO@ONKAMAL.COM
WWW.ONKAMAL.COM

0366 – 0373
ART DIRECTOR: Kamal
DESIGNER: Kamal

KATHERINE AHN
2055 RODNEY DR., #111
LOS ANGELES, CA 90027
USA
949-412-5622
KATHERINE@KATHERINEAHN.COM
WWW.KATHERINEAHN.COM

0831, 0832
DESIGNER: Katherine Ahn
CLIENT: Kate & Bryan Fry

KEVIN MCCORMICK
PENNSYLVANIA
USA
OBEYTHEKITTY@GMAIL.COM
WWW.OBEYTHEPUREBREED.COM

0711
DESIGNER: Kevin Mccormick

KIM CHAN
1648 PALM AVE.
REDWOOD CITY, CA 94061
USA
650-248-5269
KIMICHAN@GMAIL.COM
WWW.KIMCHAN.NET

0777
ART DIRECTOR: Kim Chan
DESIGNER: Kim Chan
CLIENT: Kim & Brian Hicks
ILLUSTRATOR: Hidden Villa, Los
Altos, CA

KIM KNOLL
4674 N. MANOR AVE., #3
CHICAGO, IL 60625
USA
773-756-8857
KIM@KIMKNOLL.COM
WWW.KIMKNOLL.COM

0999
ART DIRECTOR: Kim Knoll & Kyle
Eertmoed
DESIGNER: Kim Knoll & Kyle
Eertmoed
CLIENT: Self

KIRTLAND HOUSE PRESS
2025 W. SUPERIOR ST., 1F
CHICAGO, IL 60612
USA
312-206-0745
KERRIEKIRTLAND@GMAIL.COM
WWW.KIRTLANDHOUSE.COM

0365, 0375, 0376, 0378, 0379,
0834, 0860
ART DIRECTOR: Kerrie Kirtland
DESIGNER: Kerrie Kirtland
CLIENT: Kirtland House Press

LA FAMILIA GREEN
3406 W. SHAKESPEARE
CHICAGO, IL 60647
USA
773-875-7460
MOLLIE@LAFAMILIAGREEN.COM
WWW.LAFAMILIAGREEN.COM

0022, 0023, 0025
DESIGNER: Mollie Green

LAUREN MOON VEDDER
4820 PARK COMMONS DR., UNIT 236
ST. LOUIS PARK, MN 55416
USA
815-353-2989
LAURENMOON6@HOTMAIL.COM

0780
DESIGNER: Lauren Moon Vedder
CLIENT: Briton Pheffer

LEAD GRAFFITI
120A SANDY DR.
NEWARK, DE 19713
USA
302-547-6930
RAY@LEADGRAFFITI.COM
WWW.LEADGRAFFITI.COM

0178 – 0180, 0182, 0184 – 0186
ART DIRECTOR: Ray Nichols, Jill
Cypher
DESIGNER: Terre Nichols
CLIENT: Lead Graffiti

0183
ART DIRECTOR: Tray Nichols
DESIGNER: Tray Nichols
CLIENT: Tray Nichols

0187 – 0190
ART DIRECTOR: Ray Nichols, Jill
Cypher
DESIGNER: Dan Lisowski
CLIENT: Lead Graffiti

0212 – 0214
ART DIRECTOR: Ray Nichols, Jill
Cypher
DESIGNER: Chris Manson
CLIENT: Lead Graffiti

0230 – 0232
ART DIRECTOR: Ray Nichols, Jill
Cypher
DESIGNER: Sid Steinberg, Ray
Nichols, Jill Cypher
CLIENT: Lead Graffiti

0795, 0807, 0842, 0971
ART DIRECTOR: Ray Nichols, Jill
Cypher
DESIGNER: Ray Nichols, Jill Cypher
CLIENT: Lead Graffiti

LILLY & LOUISE
2925 PASEO DEL REFUGIO
SANTA BARBARA, CA 93105
USA
805-687-9414
LESLIE@LILLYANDLOUISE.COM
WWW.LILLYANDLOUISE.COM

0868
ART DIRECTOR: Leslie Lewis Sigler
DESIGNER: Leslie Lewis Sigler
CLIENT: Morgan & Heather
Simpson

LITTLE JACKET
150 PENN AVE.
SALEM, OH 44460
USA
800-433-1288
JAMIE@CRANKYPRESSMAN.COM
WWW.CRANKYPRESSMAN.COM;
WWW.LITTLE-JACKET.COM

0588
ART DIRECTOR: Jamie Berger
CLIENT: Cranky Pressman
ILLUSTRATOR: Kelly Dorsey

0589
ART DIRECTOR: Jamie Berger
CLIENT: Cranky Pressman
ILLUSTRATOR: Joey Parlett

0590
ART DIRECTOR: Jamie Berger
DESIGNER: Mickey Burton
CLIENT: Cranky Pressman

LODGE
7 JOHNSON AVE.
INDIANAPOLIS, IN 46219
USA
317-375-4399
JHAGY@LODGEDESIGN.COM
WWW.LODGEDESIGN.COM

0917, 0988
ART DIRECTOR: Eric Stine
CLIENT: Penrod Society

LYNNE DOOR
314 CORLA MIRA VISTA
SAN CLEMENTE, CA 92673
USA
949-632-6659
LDOOR@COR.NET
WWW.LYNNEDOOR.COM

0618
ART DIRECTOR: Lynne Door
DESIGNER: Lynne Door
CLIENT: GFDG

MANUEL OLMO / OLMOCS
EL CENTROL BUILDING, SUITE 215
SAN JUAN, P.R. 00918-4317
USA
787-756-4075
OLMOCS@YAHOO.COM
WWW.OLMOCS.COM

0448, 0455
ART DIRECTOR: Manuel Olmo /
Olmocs
DESIGNER: Manuel Olmo / Olmocs
CLIENT: Self

M-ART
7902 FLOWER AVE.
TACOMA PARK, MD 20912
USA
301-551-5122
MARTY@M-ART.ORG
WWW.M-ART.ORG

0469
DESIGNER: Marty Ittner
CLIENT: m-Art

0839
DESIGNER: Marty Ittner
CLIENT: Marty Ittner and Keith
Berner

ME STUDIO
KOGGESTRAAT 9M
1012 TA AMSTERDAM
THE NETHERLANDS
LOOK@MESTUDIO.INFO
WWW.MESTUDIO.INFO

0625
ART DIRECTOR: Martin Pyper
DESIGNER: Martin Pyper
CLIENT: Martin + Femke

MENAGERIE CREATIVE
18301 IRVINE BLVD.
TUSTIN, CA 92780
USA
714-731-3933
CSAVALA@MENAGERIECREATIVE.COM
WWW.MENAGERIECREATIVE.COM

0453
ART DIRECTOR: Cheryl Savala
DESIGNER: Cheryl Savala
CLIENT: Self

METALMOTHER
474 HENRY ST.
BROOKLYN, NY 11231
USA
917-613-5596
MATT@METALMOTHER.COM
WWW.METALMOTHER.COM

0791
ART DIRECTOR: Matt Dorfman
DESIGNER: Matt Dorfman
CLIENT: Jill Bell/Matt Dorfman

METHANE STUDIOS
2382 WOODACRES RD.
ATLANTA, GA 30345
USA
678-576-5432
ROBERT@METHANESTUDIOS.COM
WWW.METHANESTUDIOS.COM

0718, 0739, 0751
ART DIRECTOR: Methane Studios
DESIGNER: Robert Lee
CLIENT: OK/Windstorm Productions

0719, 0740, 0742, 0745
ART DIRECTOR: Methane Studios
DESIGNER: Robert Lee
CLIENT: OK Productions

0728
ART DIRECTOR: Methane Studios
DESIGNER: Robert Lee
CLIENT: Perpetual Groove

0737
ART DIRECTOR: Methane Studios
DESIGNER: Robert Lee
CLIENT: Phish

0738
ART DIRECTOR: Methane Studios
DESIGNER: Robert Lee
CLIENT: Methane Studios

0741, 0755
ART DIRECTOR: Methane Studios
DESIGNER: Mark McDevitt
CLIENT: Methane Studios

0743
ART DIRECTOR: Methane Studios
DESIGNER: Robert Lee
CLIENT: Stomp and Stammer
Magazine

0744
ART DIRECTOR: Methane Studios
DESIGNER: Mark McDevitt
CLIENT: Sonic Youth

0746
ART DIRECTOR: Methane Studios
DESIGNER: Robert Lee
CLIENT: Alamo Drafthouse

0747, 0756, 0757
ART DIRECTOR: Methane Studios
DESIGNER: Robert Lee
CLIENT: Dave Matthews Band

0748
ART DIRECTOR: Methane Studios
DESIGNER: Robert Lee
CLIENT: Live Nation

0749
ART DIRECTOR: Methane Studios
DESIGNER: Mark McDevitt
CLIENT: Dinosaur Jr.

0750
ART DIRECTOR: Methane Studios
DESIGNER: Mark McDevitt
CLIENT: OK Productions

0752
ART DIRECTOR: Methane Studios
DESIGNER: Mark McDevitt
CLIENT: Monsters of Folk

0753
ART DIRECTOR: Methane Studios
DESIGNER: Mark McDevitt
CLIENT: Mogwai

MICHAEL OSBORNE DESIGN
444 DE HARO ST., SUITE 207
SAN FRANCISCO, CA 94107
USA
415-255-0125
SK@MODSF.COM
WWW.MODSF.COM

0906
ART DIRECTOR: Michael Osborne
DESIGNER: Cody Dingle
CLIENT: Smithsonian National
Postal Museum

**MICHAEL OSBORNE DESIGN AND
JOEY'S CORNER**
444 DE HARO ST., SUITE 207
SAN FRANCISCO, CA 94107
USA
415-255-0125
SK@MODSF.COM
WWW.MODSF.COM; WWW.
JOEYSCORNER.ORG

0472
ART DIRECTOR: Michael Osborne
DESIGNER: Michael Osborne
CLIENT: Michael Osborne Design
and Joey's Corner

MILCH DESIGN GMBH
BAADERSTR. 19
80469 MÜNCHEN
GERMANY
089-520466-14
MARIANA_WOLFSCHOO@MILCH-
DESIGN.DE
WWW.MILCH-DESIGN.DE

0452
ART DIRECTOR: Friedel Patzak
DESIGNER: Veronika Günther
CLIENT: Grip AG

MILES DESIGN
9229 DELEGATES ROW, SUITE 460
INDIANAPOLIS, IN 46240
USA
317-915-8693
BRIAN@MILESDESIGN.COM
WWW.MILESDESIGN.COM

0432
DESIGNER: Brian K. Gray
CLIENT: Miles Design

MINDSEYE CREATIVE
21B ANAND PARSHON, 13 PEDDAR R.,
MUMBAI 400026
INDIA
91 99301 21161
UTTARA.SHAH@MECSTUDIO.COM
WWW.MECSTUDIO.COM

0872
ART DIRECTOR: Uttara Shah
DESIGNER: Uttara Shah
CLIENT: Alka/Mahendra

0963
ART DIRECTOR: Uttara Shah
DESIGNER: Uttara Shah
CLIENT: Abhi Shek/Debbie

0967
ART DIRECTOR: Uttara Shah
DESIGNER: Shashank Pattear
CLIENT: H. Dipak

MIRIELLO GRAFICO
1660 LOGAN AVE.
SAN DIEGO, CA 92113
USA
619-234-1124
LAUREN@MIRIELLOGRAFICO.COM
WWW.MIRIELLOGRAFICO.COM

0570
ART DIRECTOR: Ron Miriello,
Dennis Garcia
DESIGNER: Dennis Garcia, Tracy
Meiers, Robert Palmer, Justin
Skeesuck, Sallie Reynolds-Allen
CLIENT: Fox River Paper/Miriello
Grafico

0593
ART DIRECTOR: Ron Miriello
DESIGNER: Dennis Garcia, Tracy
Meiners, Christine Nguyen
CLIENT: Self

MOAG BAILIE
66 DEAN ST.
NEWLANDS 7700 CAPE TOWN
SOUTH AFRICA
27 21 6851272
MOAG@MWEB.CO.SA
WWW.MOAGBAILIE.COM

0503
ART DIRECTOR: Annie Moag
DESIGNER: Tatum Cochrane
CLIENT: Moag Bailie

MOOMAH
161 HUDSON ST.
NEW YORK, NY 10013
USA
212-226-0345
JACQUELINE@MOOMAH.COM
WWW.MOOMAH.COM

0227 – 0229
ART DIRECTOR: Jacqueline Schmidt
DESIGNER: Jacqueline Schmidt

MR. FANCY PANTS
1021 E. 7TH ST., SUITE 102
AUSTIN, TX 78702
USA
903-701-6863
WILL@WILL-BRYANT.COM
WWW.WILL-BRYANT.COM

0599
DESIGNER: Will Bryant
CLIENT: Test Everything Press

0603
DESIGNER: Will Bryant

0666
DESIGNER: Will Bryant
CLIENT: Pro Bono

0675
DESIGNER: Will Bryant
CLIENT: MSU Music Makers

MY ASSOCIATE CORNELIUS
727 WOODSON LANE
GARDNER, KANSAS 66030
USA
913-486-5077
AMICAHSMITH@GMAIL.COM
WWW.MYASSOCIATECORNELIUS.COM

0500
ART DIRECTOR: A. Micah Smith
DESIGNER: A. Micah Smith
CLIENT: Self

0682, 0732
ART DIRECTOR: A. Micah Smith
DESIGNER: A. Micah Smith
CLIENT: Mates of State

0705, 0724
ART DIRECTOR: A. Micah Smith
DESIGNER: A. Micah Smith
CLIENT: Hollywood Bowl

0713
ART DIRECTOR: A. Micah Smith
DESIGNER: A. Micah Smith
CLIENT: Explosions in the Sky

0714, 0720, 0721, 0723, 0730,
0735, 0754
ART DIRECTOR: A. Micah Smith
DESIGNER: A. Micah Smith
CLIENT: Myspace Music

0715, 0731
ART DIRECTOR: A. Micah Smith
DESIGNER: A. Micah Smith
CLIENT: Wilco

0716
ART DIRECTOR: A. Micah Smith
DESIGNER: A. Micah Smith
CLIENT: Ultimate Facebook

0717, 0722, 0734
ART DIRECTOR: A. Micah Smith
DESIGNER: A. Micah Smith
CLIENT: The Get Up Kids

0726
ART DIRECTOR: A. Micah Smith
DESIGNER: A. Micah Smith
CLIENT: Andrew Bird

0729
ART DIRECTOR: A. Micah Smith
DESIGNER: A. Micah Smith
CLIENT: New Kids on the Block

0733
ART DIRECTOR: A. Micah Smith
DESIGNER: A. Micah Smith
CLIENT: Okkervil River

0736
ART DIRECTOR: A. Micah Smith
DESIGNER: A. Micah Smith
CLIENT: Coalesce

0758
ART DIRECTOR: A. Micah Smith
DESIGNER: A. Micah Smith
CLIENT: AC Newman

0804, 0818
ART DIRECTOR: A. Micah Smith
DESIGNER: A. Micah Smith

NATOOF
PO BOX 60045
DUBAI
UAE
INFO@NATOOF.COM
WWW.NATOOF.COM

0236 – 0238
ART DIRECTOR: Mariam Bin Natoof
DESIGNER: Mariam Bin Natoof
CLIENT: Consumer

0844
ART DIRECTOR: Mariam Bin Natoof
DESIGNER: Mariam Bin Natoof

NICEVENTS
275 WEBSTER AVE., 6M
BROOKLYN, NY 11230
USA
646-831-0818
EVENTS@NIC-EVENTS.NET
WWW.NIC-EVENTS.NET

0781
ART DIRECTOR: Nicole Block
DESIGNER: Nicole Block
CLIENT: Adrienne & Andrew

0848, 0852
ART DIRECTOR: Nicole Block
DESIGNER: Nicole Block
CLIENT: Betsy & Jeb

NICOLE LAVELLE
2221 SE ELLIOTT AVE.
PORTLAND, OR 97214
USA
541-554-7889
NICOLELAVELLE@GMAIL.COM
WWW.MAKINGSTUFFANDDOINGTHINGS
.COM

0567
DESIGNER: Nicole Lavelle, Sarah
Baugh
CLIENT: Friends of Graphic Design

NIGHT OWL PAPER GOODS
33 BARBER COURT, #125
BIRMINGHAM, AL 35209
USA
205-868-1619
INFO@NIGHTOWLPAPERGOODS.COM
WWW.NIGHTOWLPAPERGOODS.COM

0299 – 0308
DESIGNER: Jennifer Tatham
CLIENT: Night Owl Paper Goods

OBERLANDER GROUP
143 REMSEN
COHOES, NY 12047
USA
518-720-0050 X 233
LALLARD@OBERLANDERGROUP.COM
WWW.OBERLANDERGROUP.COM

0969
ART DIRECTOR: Ruth Sadinsky
DESIGNER: Ruth Sadinsky

0983
ART DIRECTOR: Flo Luckey
DESIGNER: Flo Luckey
CLIENT: Rensselear Polytechnic
Institute

OBLATION PAPERS + PRESS
516 N.W. 12TH AVE.
PORTLAND, OR 97209
USA
503-295-5967
VANESSA@OBLATIONPAPERS.COM
WWW.OBLATIONPAPERS.COM

**0398, 0399, 0417 – 0425, 0617,
0787**
ART DIRECTOR: Ron + Jennifer Rich
DESIGNER: Mayumi Schatz,
Jennifer Rich, Ben Verhoeven,
Ron Rich

OCTAVIUS MURRAY
57 HEMINGFORD RD.
LONDON N1 1BY
UK
OCKY@COGDESIGN.COM

0416
ART DIRECTOR: Octavius Murray
DESIGNER: Octavius Murray
CLIENT: Octavius Murray

OH JOY!
254 C AVE.
CORONADO, CA 92118
USA
215-200-6578
HELLO@OHJOY.COM
WWW.OHJOY.COM

0007 – 0010
ART DIRECTOR: Joy Cho
DESIGNER: Joy Cho
CLIENT: Oh Joy!

0830
ART DIRECTOR: Joy Cho
DESIGNER: Joy Cho
CLIENT: Jane Song

ORANGE SPOT PINK NOSE
2701 W. 15TH, #509
PLANO, TX 75075
USA
972-422-9513
LEANNE@ORANGESPOTPINKNOSE.COM
WWW.ORANGESPOTPINKNOSE.COM

0820
DESIGNER: Leanne Sutton
CLIENT: Diamond Affairs

0886
ART DIRECTOR:
DESIGNER: Leanne Sutton
CLIENT: American Airlines C.R.
Smith Museum

ORANGEBEAUTIFUL
1700 W. IRVING PARK RD.,
SUITE 305B
MINNEAPOLIS, MN 55414
USA
773-975-3570
INFO@STUDIOONFIRE.COM
WWW.STUDIOONFIRE.COM

**0003 – 0006, 0098, 0172 –
0177, 0339 – 0342, 0387, 0855**

P22 TYPE FOUNDRY
PO BOX 770
BUFFALO, NY 14213
USA
716-885-4490
RICHARD@P22.COM
WWW.P22.COM

0437
ART DIRECTOR: Richard Kegler
DESIGNER: Richard Kegler
CLIENT: P22 Type Foundry

PANCAKE & FRANKS
352 LEXINGTON ST.
SAN FRANCISCO, CA 94110
USA
415-642-7667
INFO@PANCAKEANDFRANKS.COM
WWW.PANCAKEANDFRANKS.COM

0221, 0226
DESIGNER: Stacy Pancake

0851
DESIGNER: Stacy Pancake
CLIENT: Bride and Groom (Peters
and North)

PAPER RELICS
9826 BAYLINE CIRCLE
OWINGS MILLS, MD 21117
USA
410-599-7401
HOPE@PAPERRELICS.COM
WWW.PAPERRELICS.COM

0209 – 0211, 0216 – 0218
DESIGNER: Hope Wallace Karney
CLIENT: Paper Relics

PAPER SCHMAPER
USA
314-229-3479
KRISSY@KRISSYERKMANN.COM
WWW.PAPERSCHMAPER.COM

0361, 0362, 0377, 0380
DESIGNER: Krissy Erkmann
CLIENT: Personal

**PARAGON MARKETING
COMMUNICATIONS**
SALMIYA, SALEM AL-MUBARAK
STREET, AL-FANOR MALL, 1ST
FLOOR, OFF. 21 J
P.O. BOX 6097 SALMIYA 22071
KUWAIT
(965) 25716063-25716068-
25716039
INFO@PARAGONMC.COM
WWW.PARAGONMC.COM

0436
ART DIRECTOR: Louai Alasfahani
CLIENT: Alwasata National
Financial Co.

0443
ART DIRECTOR: Louai Alasfahani
CLIENT: Salhiya Complex

0482
ART DIRECTOR: Konstantin
Assenov
CLIENT: Tarasul Telecom

PENCIL
35 GAY ST.
BATH, BA1 2NT
UK
0845 290 3930
LUKE@PENCILUK.CO.UK
WWW.PENCILUK.CO.UK

0561, 0616
ART DIRECTOR: Luke Manning
DESIGNER: Luke Manning
CLIENT: Pencil

PEPPERSPROUTS
295 KINGSLAND AVE., APT. #3
BROOKLYN, NY 11222
USA
718-473-6363
PEPPERSPROUTS@GMAIL.COM
WWW.PEPPERSPROUTDESIGNS.COM

0485
ART DIRECTOR: Jen Pepper
DESIGNER: Jen Pepper
CLIENT: Self-promotion

PERKY BROS LLC
1200 CLINTON ST., SUITE 221
NASHVILLE, TN 37203
USA
615-760-5568
JEFF@PERKYBROS.COM
WWW.PERKYBROS.,COM

0786
ART DIRECTOR: Jefferson Perky
DESIGNER: Jefferson Perky

PILLAR IN-HOUSE CREATIVE
1894 GILLIAN WAY
SAN JOSE, CA 95132
USA
408-202-4945
JENN@JOYDESIGN.US

0465
ART DIRECTOR: Kevin Perera
DESIGNER: Jenn Zuverink
CLIENT: Pillar Data Systems

PISCATELLO DESIGN CENTRE
330 W. 38TH ST.
NEW YORK, NY 10018
USA
212-502-4734
ROCCO@PISCATELLO.COM
WWW.PISCATELLO.COM

0655, 0656
DESIGNER: Rocco Piscatello
CLIENT: Fashion Institute of
Technology

PLAZM
PO BOX 2863
PORTLAND, OR 97208
USA
JOSH@PLAZM.COM
WWW.PLAZM.COM

0388
ART DIRECTOR: Joshua Berger
DESIGNER: Brendan Miller
illustration: Patrick Long

POP + SHORTY
205 HOLTZCLAW ST., UNIT E
ATLANTA, GA 30316
USA
323-369-1514
POPANDSHORTY@ME.COM
WWW.POPANDSHORTY.COM

0090, 0160, 0196, 0198, 0203, 0242
ART DIRECTOR: Ashley Dailey
DESIGNER: Ashley Dailey

PRODUCT SUPERIOR LTD.
13217 MISTY SAGE DR.
CONROE, TX 77302
USA
347-743-7621
JENNIFER@PRODUCTSUPERIOR
.COM
WWW.PRODUCTSUPERIOR.COM

0151, 0154, 0156, 0158, 0159, 0615
ART DIRECTOR: Jennifer Blanco
DESIGNER: John Earles,
Jennifer Blanco

0152, 0153, 0155, 0157
ART DIRECTOR: Jennifer Blanco
DESIGNER: Jennifer Blanco, John
Earles

PUP & PONY PRESS
269 ROYCROFT AVE.
LONG BEACH, CA 90803
USA
562-434-7815
WENDY@PUPANDPONY.COM
WWW.PUPANDPONY.COM

0065, 0067, 0142 – 0144, 0149, 0150
ART DIRECTOR: Wendy Emery
DESIGNER: Wendy Emery

PYLON
171 EAST LIBERTY ST., SUITE 204
TORONTO, ON M6K 3P6
CANADA
416-504-4331
LIAM@PYLON.CA
WWW.PYLON.CA

0463, 0481

R DESIGN
420 HIGHGATE STUDIOS, 53-79
HIGHGATE RD.
LONDON NW5 1TL
UK
DAVE@R-EMAIL.CO.UK
WWW.R-DESIGN.CO.UK

0468
ART DIRECTOR: Dave Richmond
DESIGNER: Sian Sargent
CLIENT: R Design
ILLUSTRATOR: Rosie Buckler

0489
ART DIRECTOR: Dave Richmond
CLIENT: R Design

0552, 0580
ART DIRECTOR: Dave Richmond
DESIGNER: Dave Richmond
CLIENT: R Design

0558
ART DIRECTOR: Dave Richmond
DESIGNER: Sian Sargent
CLIENT: R Design

RAMP CREATIVE
411 S. MAIN ST., SUITE 615
LOS ANGELES, CA 90013
USA
213-623-7267
MICHAEL@RAMPCREATIVE.COM
WWW.RAMPCREATIVE.COM

0890
ART DIRECTOR: Michael Stinson
DESIGNER: Michael Stinson
CLIENT: CWS Capital Partners

RECHERCHÉ INVITATIONS
12 HALIFAX PLACE
IRVINE, CA 92602
USA
714-352-6432
INFO@RECHERCHEINVITATIONS.COM
WWW.RECHERCHEINVITATIONS.COM

0829
ART DIRECTOR: Courtney Jacques
DESIGNER: Courtney Jacques
CLIENT: Courtney Jacques

0843
ART DIRECTOR: Courtney Jacques
DESIGNER: Courtney Jacques
CLIENT: Stephanie Chandler

0846
ART DIRECTOR: Courtney Jacques
DESIGNER: Courtney Jacques
CLIENT: Jenia Crockett

REDBEAN DESIGN
582 GROVE ST., #11
SAN FRANCISCO, CA 94102
USA
415-630-0618
MELISSA@REDBEAN.COM
WWW.REDBEAN.COM

0483
ART DIRECTOR: Melissa Crowley
DESIGNER: Melissa Crowley
CLIENT: Redbean Design

REICH + PETCH
1867 YONGE ST., SUITE 1100
TORONTO, ON M45 1Y5
CANADA
416-480-2020
CHOW@REICH-PETCH.COM
WWW.REICH-PETCH.COM

0943
ART DIRECTOR: Edmund Li
DESIGNER: Nancy Ng
CLIENT: Reich + Petch

REPEAT PRESS
9 OLIVE SQ.
SOMERVILLE, MA 02143
USA
781-962-4834
MIKE@REPEATPRESS.COM
WWW.REPEATPRESS.COM

0492
DESIGNER: Repeat Press
CLIENT: Titel Media

RIFLE PAPER CO.
704 W. FAIRBANKS AVE.
WINTER PARK, FL 32789
USA
407-622-7679
INFO@RIFLEPAPERCO.COM
WWW.RIFLEPAPERCO.COM

0061 – 0062, 0244 – 0250, 0360, 0363, 0364, 0805, 0809, 0811 – 0815

RIPPLE MARKETING
PO BOX 10221
BOZEMAN, MT 59719
USA
406-585-8168
KURT@RIPPLEMARKETING.COM
WWW.RIPPLEMARKETING.COM

0894
ART DIRECTOR: Kurt Palmquist
DESIGNER: Bryan Hintz
CLIENT: Bozeman Deaconess
Foundation

ROME & GOLD CREATIVE
1305 TIJERAS AVE. NW
ALBUQUERQUE, NM 87102
USA
505-897-0870
LORENZO@RGCREATIVE.COM
WWW.RGCREATIVE.COM

0568
ART DIRECTOR: Lorenzo Romero
DESIGNER: Lorenzo Romero,
Carlos Bobadilla
CLIENT: Rome & Gold Creative

0604
ART DIRECTOR: Lorenzo Romero
DESIGNER: Lorenzo Romero,
Carlos Bobadilla
CLIENT: New Mexico Advertising
Federation

ROOT STUDIO
THE TERRACE, GRANTHAM ST.
LINCOLN, ENGLAND
UK
01522 528246
DESIGN@ROOTSTUDIO.CO.UK
WWW.ROOTSTUDIO.CO.UK

0783
ART DIRECTOR: Lydia Sibson
DESIGNER: Tom Bradley
CLIENT: Lydia + Tom

ROUGHSTOCK STUDIOS
PO BOX 460010
SAN FRANCISCO, CA 94146
USA
415-643-0121
JSAND@ROUGHSTOCKSTUDIOS.COM
WWW.ROUGHSTOCKSTUDIOS.COM

0602
DESIGNER: Jess Sand
CLIENT: San Francisco Green
Business Week

RUBBER DESIGN
375 ALABAMA ST., SUITE 228
SAN FRANCISCO, CA 94110
USA
415-626-2990
JACQUIE@RUBBERDESIGN.COM
WWW.RUBBERDESIGN.COM

0600
DESIGNER: Jacquie Van Keuren,
Will Yarbrough, Ian Gordon
CLIENT: New Leaf Paper &
Paragraphics

**RUBY VICTORIA LETTERPRESS +
PRINTMAKING**
39 ILLAWARRA CT.
BLACKMANS BAY TAS 7052
AUSTRALIA
03-62293851
RUBY-NELL@HOTMAIL.COM
WWW.ETSY.COM/SHOP/
RUBYVICTORIA

0075, 0080, 0381
DESIGNER: N. Badalassi
CLIENT: Market + Online Stores

RULE 29
501 HAMILTON ST.
GENEVA, IL 60134
USA
630-262-1009
KATRINA@RULE29.COM
WWW.RULE29.COM

0431
ART DIRECTOR: Justin Ahrens
DESIGNER: Susan Herda
CLIENT: Rule 29

0597
ART DIRECTOR: Justin Ahrens
DESIGNER: Tim Damitz
CLIENT: Rule 29

RUTH HUIMERIND
RANNAKU PST 9-29
10917 TALLINN
ESTONIA
372 511501
ROSA.PERMANENTE@MAIL.EE
WWW.RUTHHUIMERIND.COM

0059
ART DIRECTOR: Ruth Huimerind
DESIGNER: Jyri Loun
CLIENT: Lakrito Printing House

0470
ART DIRECTOR: Ruth Huimerind
DESIGNER: Ruth Huimerind
CLIENT: Ruth Huimerind

SAGMEISTER INC.
266 W. 23RD ST, FOURTH FLOOR
NEW YORK CITY, NY 10011
USA
212-647-1789
INFO@SAGMEISTER.COM
WWW.SAGMEISTER.COM

0574
ART DIRECTOR: Stefan Sagmeister
DESIGNER: Joe Shouldice,
Richard The
ILLUSTRATION: Nick Dewar, Jared
Stone, Mark Pernice

0581, 0582
ART DIRECTOR: Stefan Sagmeister
DESIGNER: Joe Shouldice
CLIENT: Anni Kuan

0635
ART DIRECTOR: Stefan Sagmeister
DESIGNER: Mark Pernice

SAINT BERNADINE MISSION
802-318 HOMER ST.
VANCOUVER, BC V6B 2V2
CANADA
604-646-0001
DWALKER@STBERNADINE.COM
WWW.STBERNADINE.COM

0858
ART DIRECTOR: David Walker,
Andrew Samuel
DESIGNER: Olga Gryb
CLIENT: Mr. & Mrs. Waldman

SCREECH OWL DESIGN
59 GREEN ST.
BROOKLYN, NY 11222
USA
718-702-7556
JS@SCREECHOWLDESIGN.COM
WWW.SCREECHOWLDESIGN.COM

0013, 0014, 0016 – 0018
ART DIRECTOR: Jacqueline Schmidt
DESIGNER: Jacqueline Schmidt

SELTZER DESIGN
PO BOX 470802
BROOKLINE, MA 02447
USA
617-353-0303
PROJECT@SELTZERDESIGN.COM
WWW.SELTZERDESIGN.COM

0928
ART DIRECTOR: Rochelle Seltzer
DESIGNER: Rochelle Seltzer
CLIENT: Gabriel Seltzer

SELTZER, LLC
37-24 24TH ST., #412
LONG ISLAND CITY, NY 11101
USA
718-752-1533
GAY@SELTZERGOODS.COM
WWW.SELTZERGOODS.COM

**0012, 0015, 0019 – 0021, 0027,
0029, 0030, 0032, 0034, 0036,
0038, 0191 – 0195, 0557**
ART DIRECTOR: Brian Gold, Gay
W. Lam
DESIGNER: Brian Gold, Gay W. Lam

SERAPH DESIGN
20900 N.E. 30TH AVE., SUITE 818
AVENTURA, FL 33180
USA
305-438-7697
STEPHANIE@SERAPHMIAMI.COM
WWW.SERAPHMIAMI.COM

0427
ART DIRECTOR: Stephanie Tisch
DESIGNER: Johanna Bjork
CLIENT: Turnberry Ltd.

0968
ART DIRECTOR: Stephanie Tisch
DESIGNER: Johanna Bjork
CLIENT: Carnival Center For The
Performing Arts

0991, 0995
ART DIRECTOR: Stephanie Tisch
CLIENT: Related Group

**SERIES NEMO. BRAND GRAPHICS
& PACKAGING**
C/ RAMÓN TURRÓ 23, 6TH FLOOR
BARCELONA
SPAIN
0034 93 221 18 27
INFO@SERIESNEMO.COM
WWW.SERIESNEMO.COM
WWW.SERIESD.COM

0535
DESIGNER: Series Nemo Team
CLIENT: Self

SET EDITIONS
PO BOX 1314
HUDSON, NY 12534
USA
917-714-0564
RILEY@SETEDITIONS.COM
WWW.SETEDITIONS.COM

0441, 0508, 0622
ART DIRECTOR: Alison Riley
DESIGNER: Alison Riley
CLIENT: Set Editions

**SEVEN25. DESIGN &
TYPOGRAPHY**
309E-896 CAMBIE STREET
VANCOUVER, BC V6B 2P6
CANADA
1-604-685-0097
STUDIO@SEVEN25.COM
WWW.SEVEN25.COM

0636, 0982
ART DIRECTOR: Isabelle Swiderski
DESIGNER: Isabelle Swiderski
CLIENT: Seven 25. Design &
Typography

SHAUNA CROSS DESIGN
610 SCOTTSVILLE CHILI RD.
SCOTTSVILLE, NY 14546
USA
585-732-5376
SHAUNA@SHAUNACROSS.COM
WWW.SHAUNACROSS.COM

0854
ART DIRECTOR: Shauna Cross
CLIENT: David Tutera

0876, 0878
ART DIRECTOR: Shauna Cross

SHELBY DESIGNS & ILLUSTRATES
155 FILBERT ST., SUITE 216
OAKLAND, CA 94607
USA
510-444-0502
SUPPORT@SHELBYDESIGNS.COM
WWW.SHELBYDESIGNS.COM

0510
ART DIRECTOR: Shelby Putnam
Tupper
DESIGNER: Will Yang
CLIENT: Shelby Designs & Illustrates

0583
ART DIRECTOR: Shelby Putnam
Tupper
DESIGNER: Donna Castro, Tae
Hatayama
CLIENT: Shelby Designs & Illustrates

SHE'S SO CREATIVE
1824 CENTRO WEST ST., UNIT A
TIBURON, CA 94920
USA
415-328-5993
HELLO@SHESOCREATIVE.COM
WWW.SHESOCREDATIVE.COM

0068 – 0074
ART DIRECTOR: Stephanie Orma
DESIGNER: Stephanie Orma

SIDESHOW PRESS
9 CANNON ST.
CHARLESTON, SC 29403
USA
843-722-6296
COURTNEY@SIDESHOWPRESS.COM
WWW.SIDESHOWPRESS.COM

0624
ART DIRECTOR: Amy Pastre
CLIENT: Otto Pastre

0826, 0827
DESIGNER: Courtney Rowson,
Amy Pastre
CLIENT: Courtney Pakis

0867
DESIGNER: Amy Pastre, Courtney
Rowson
CLIENT: Halle Lipon

0881
DESIGNER: Courtney Rowson
CLIENT: Sally Bea Rowson

0882, 0883
DESIGNER: Courtney Rowson,
Amy Pastre
CLIENT: Franca Lynch

0884
DESIGNER: Amy Pastre, Courtney
Rowson
CLIENT: Lowcountry Local First

0885
DESIGNER: Courtney Rowson,
Amy Pastre
CLIENT: Alyssa Worsham

0899
DESIGNER: Courtney Rowson,
Amy Pastre
CLIENT: Renee Lubelli

0901, 0905
DESIGNER: Courtney Rowson
CLIENT: Eric Hobgeod

0903
DESIGNER: Amy Pastre, Courtney
Rowson
CLIENT: Sarah Chanlan

0929
DESIGNER: Amy Pastre
CLIENT: Courtney Rowson

0953
DESIGNER: Courtney Rowson,
Amy Pastre
CLIENT: Lee Bros.

0974
DESIGNER: Amy Pastre, Courtney
Rowson
CLIENT: The Priloves

0981
DESIGNER: Amy Pastre, Courtney
Rowson
CLIENT: High South Carolina

0996
DESIGNER: Courtney Rowson,
Amy Pastre
CLIENT: Franca Lynch

**SIMON & GOETZ DESIGN GMBH
& CO. KG**
WIESENAU 27-29
60323 FRANKFURT/MAIN
GERMANY
49 (0)69 968855-0
B.VOLLMOLLER@SIMONGOETZ.DE
WWW.SIMONGOETZ.DE

0505
ART DIRECTOR: Bernd Vollmöller
DESIGNER: Juliana Kromberg,
Bernd Vollmöller
CLIENT: Simon & Goetz Design

SIQUIS
1340 SMITH AVE., SUITE 300
BALTIMORE, MD 21209
USA
410-353-4800
GREG@SIQUIS.COM
WWW.SIQUIS.COM

0621
ART DIRECTOR: Greg Bennett
DESIGNER: Greg Bennett
CLIENT: Jamie Kaplan and
Russell Green

SK+G
8912 SPANISH RIDGE AVE.
LAS VEGAS, NV 89178
USA
702-478-4114
JEREMY.BRISTOL@SKGADV.COM
BELLE.LARSEN@SKGADV.COM
WWW.SKGADV.COM

0659
ART DIRECTOR: Steve Averitt
DESIGNER: Iris Morales
CLIENT: Fisy Camp

0873
ART DIRECTOR: Steve Averitt
DESIGNER: Tracy Brockhouse,
Alex Smith
CLIENT: Montage

0887
ART DIRECTOR: Steve Averitt
DESIGNER: Iris Morales
CLIENT: Louis's

0932
ART DIRECTOR: Jeremy Bristol
DESIGNER: Becca Rios
CLIENT: Palms, Las Vegas

0946
ART DIRECTOR: Steve Averitt
DESIGNER: Belle Larsen
CLIENT: Nevada Cancer Institute

0960
ART DIRECTOR: Jeremy Bristol
DESIGNER: Monica Maccaux
CLIENT: The Water Club at Borgata

0961
ART DIRECTOR: Jeremy Bristol
DESIGNER: Marshall Aune
CLIENT: The Borgata, Atlantic City

0965
ART DIRECTOR: Steve Averitt
DESIGNER: Joe Boswell
CLIENT: Nevada Cancer Institute

0966
ART DIRECTOR: Jeremy Bristol
DESIGNER: Monica Maccaux
CLIENT: The Water Club at Borgata

0970
ART DIRECTOR: Jeremy Bristol
DESIGNER: Nick West
CLIENT: The Water Club at Borgata

0993
ART DIRECTOR: Jeremy Bristol
DESIGNER: Becca Rios
CLIENT: Mandarin Oriental, Las Vegas

0994
ART DIRECTOR: Jeremy Bristol
DESIGNER: Becca Rios, Carl Medley
CLIENT: Aria, Las Vegas

SPLASH PRODUCTIONS PTE LTD
114 BUKIT MERAH VIEW
#01-590, SINGAPORE 150114
SINGAPORE
65 6396 8438
STANLEY@SPLASH.SG
WWW.SPLASH.SG

0670 – 0673
ART DIRECTOR: Stanley Yap
DESIGNER: Natalie Low
CLIENT: Splash Productions Pte Ltd

STATUS SERIGRAPH
3352 KENILWORTH LN.
KNOXVILLE, TN 37917
USA
865-591-6522
STATUS_SERIGRAPH@HOTMAIL.COM
WWW.STATUSSERIGRAPH.COM

0689
ART DIRECTOR: Justin Helton
DESIGNER: Justin Helton
CLIENT: The Decemberists

0691
ART DIRECTOR: Justin Helton
DESIGNER: Justin Helton
CLIENT: North Mississippi All Stars

0692
ART DIRECTOR: Justin Helton
DESIGNER: Justin Helton
CLIENT: RJD2

0693
ART DIRECTOR: Justin Helton
DESIGNER: Justin Helton
CLIENT: Clearchannel Radio

0694
ART DIRECTOR: Justin Helton
DESIGNER: Justin Helton
CLIENT: Ween

0695
ART DIRECTOR: Justin Helton
DESIGNER: Justin Helton
CLIENT: Yonder Mountain String Band

STUDIO ON FIRE
1621 E. HENNEPIN AVE., #226
MINNEAPOLIS, MN 55414
USA
612-379-3000
INFO@STUDIOONFIRE.COM
WWW.STUDIOONFIRE.COM

0493, 0495 – 0497

SUBSTANCE151
2304 E. BALTIMORE ST.
BALTIMORE, MD 21224
USA
410-732-8379
IDA@SUBSTANCE151.COM
WWW.SUBSTANCE151.COM

0585
ART DIRECTOR: Ida Cheinman
DESIGNER: Ida Cheinman, Rick Salzman
CLIENT: substance151

SUGAR RIVER STATIONERS
7770 NOLL VALLEY RD.
VERONA, WI 53593
USA
608-798-0427
INFO@SUGARRIVERSTATIONERS.COM
WWW.SUGARRIVERSTATIONERS.COM

0819
ART DIRECTOR: Heather Martens-Raffel
DESIGNER: Heather Martens-Raffel
CLIENT: Amy Siegel

0869
ART DIRECTOR: Heather Martens-Raffel
DESIGNER: Heather Martens-Raffel
CLIENT: UWHA

SWEETBEAKER
2264 BYRON COURT
MARIETTA, GA 30064
USA
404-309-1897
SWEETBEAKER@GMAIL.COM
WWW.SWEETBEAKER.COM

0788
ART DIRECTOR: Karly A. Young
DESIGNER: Karly A. Young
CLIENT: Thomas + Kelley Chambers

SYCAMORE STREET PRESS
904 S. 300W
HEBER CITY, UT 84032
USA
614-949-3023
EVA@SYCAMORESTREETPRESS.COM
WWW.SYCAMORESTREETPRESS.COM

0082, 0083, 0181, 0215
DESIGNER: Kristin Mills, Amy Shaffer
CLIENT: Sycamore Street Press

0084, 0085
DESIGNER: Eva Jorgensen
CLIENT: Sycamore Street Press

SYNERGY GRAPHIX
210 E. 49TH ST., 2ND FLOOR
NEW YORK, NY 10017
USA
646-442-1000
RSTRADA@SYNERGYGRAPHIX.COM

0623
ART DIRECTOR: Remo Strada
DESIGNER: Remo Strada
CLIENT: Remo & Elaine Strada

0980
ART DIRECTOR: Remo Strada
DESIGNER: Remo Strada
CLIENT: Reservoir Capital

TAD CARPENTER/VAHALLA
523 GRAND #4E
KANSAS CITY, MO 64106
USA
913-302-1019
TAD@TADCARPENTER.COM

0271 – 0275, 0317, 0322 – 0330, 0334 – 0338, 0725, 0759 – 0773

THE CARTE POSTALE
24 PRIORY GROVE
LONDON SW82 P18
UK
0770 300 11 56
PHIL@THECARTEPOSTALE.COM

0347 – 0353
ART DIRECTOR: Philippe Ruso
DESIGNER: Keith Stephenson

THE CREATIVE METHOD
STUDIO 10-50 RESERVOIR STREET
SURRY HILLS, NSW 2010
AUSTRALIA
6128231 9977
JESS@THECREATIVEMETHOD.COM
WWW.THECREATIVEMETHOD.COM

0945
ART DIRECTOR: Tony Ibbotson
DESIGNER: Andi Yanto
CLIENT: The Creative Method

0949
ART DIRECTOR: Tony Ibbotson
DESIGNER: Mayra Monobe
CLIENT: The Creative Method

THE HIVE DESIGN STUDIO
571 SKYPARK DR.
SCOTTS VALLEY, CA; SANTA CRUZ, CA; MADISON, WI
USA
831-440-1983
LAURIE.OKAMURA@COMCAST.NET
WWW.LUCKYBEEPRESS.ETSY.NET

0161, 0162, 0164 – 0166, 0202
ART DIRECTOR: Laurie Okamura, Amy Stocklein
DESIGNER: Laurie Olamura
CLIENT: Lucky Bee Press

0163
ART DIRECTOR: Laurie Okamura, Amy Stocklein
DESIGNER: Amy Stocklein
CLIENT: Lucky Bee Press

THE JONES GROUP
342 MARIETTA ST., SUITE 3
ATLANTA, GA 30313
USA
404-523-2606
MIRANDA@THEJONESGROUP.COM
WWW.THEJONESGROUP.COM

0892
ART DIRECTOR: Kendra Lively
DESIGNER: Tifanni Spann
CLIENT: High Museum Atlanta Wine Auction

THE NBC AGENCY
30 ROCKEFELLER PLAZA
NEW YORK, NY 10112
USA
212-664-3482
MELINDA.GRAY@NBCUNI.COM
WWW.NBCUNI.COM

0606
ART DIRECTOR: Melinda Gray
DESIGNER: Melinda Gray
CLIENT: Chiller TV

0938
ART DIRECTOR: Bari Cohen
DESIGNER: Mary Jean Templin
CLIENT: NBC Universal

THE PAPER NUT
906 RIVERVIEW AVE.
SELAH, WA 98942
USA
619-339-8547
JEANIE@THEPAPERNUT.COM
WWW.THEPAPERNUT.COM

0205 – 0208
ART DIRECTOR: Jeanie Nelson
DESIGNER: Jeanie Nelson
CLIENT: The Paper Nut

0534, 0796
ART DIRECTOR: Jeanie Nelson
DESIGNER: Jeanie Nelson
CLIENT: Elaine Litchfield

0784
ART DIRECTOR: Jeanie Nelson
DESIGNER: Jeanie Nelson
CLIENT: Jessica Shulte

0793
ART DIRECTOR: Jeanie Nelson
DESIGNER: Jeanie Nelson
CLIENT: Bari Kessler

THE PERMANENT COLLECTION
5508 WESTWOOD DR.
DES MOINES, IA 50312
USA
515-255-1015
THEPERMANENTCOLLECTION@GMAIL.COM
WWW.THEPCPRESS.ETSY.COM;
THEPERMANENTCOLLECTION@GMAIL.COM

0253, 0391, 0396, 0397
ART DIRECTOR: Sarah McCoy
DESIGNER: Sarah McCoy
CLIENT: Retail & Online Sales

THOMAS MANSS & CO
3 NILE ST.
LONDON N1 7LX
UK
44(0)20 72 51 77 77
KEIRA@MANSS.COM
WWW.MANSS.COM

0473
ART DIRECTOR: Thomas Manss
CLIENT: Thomas Manss & Co

THREE STEPS AHEAD
2570 W. 235TH ST., #8
TORRANCE, CA 90505-4209
USA
310-961-4366
JOSH@THREESTEPSAHEAD.COM
WWW.THREESTEPSAHEAD.COM

0803
ART DIRECTOR: Josh Korwin, Alyssa Zukas
DESIGNER: Josh Korwin, Alyssa Zukas
CLIENT: Josh Korwin, Alyssa Zukas

THRIVE DESIGN
529 HILLCREST AVE.
EAST LANSING, MI 48823
USA
401-578-1795
KSALCHOW@AOL.COM

0789
ART DIRECTOR: Kelly Salchow
Macarthur
DESIGNER: Kelly Salchow
Macarthur
CLIENT: Raegen Salchow +
Morgan Stauffer

TIMBER DESIGN CO.
4402 NORTH COLLEGE AVE.
INDIANAPOLIS, INDIANA 46205
USA
317-213-8509
LARS@TIMBERDESIGNCO.COM
WWW.TIMBERDESIGNCO.COM

0438 – 0440, 0922, 0940
ART DIRECTOR: Lars Lawson
DESIGNER: Lars Lawson
CLIENT: Timber Design Co.

0607
ART DIRECTOR: Lars Lawson
DESIGNER: Lars Lawson
CLIENT: Mine Storage

0660
ART DIRECTOR: Lars Larson
DESIGNER: Lars Larson
CLIENT: Indianapolis Ad Club

0661 – 0663
ART DIRECTOR: Lars Larson
DESIGNER: Lars Larson
CLIENT: Indianapolis Ad Club

0864
ART DIRECTOR: Lars Lawson
DESIGNER: Lars Lawson
CLIENT: Jim Tomlinson

0877
ART DIRECTOR: Lars Lawson
DESIGNER: Lars Lawson
CLIENT: 8Fifteen

0925
ART DIRECTOR: Lars Lawson
DESIGNER: Lars Lawson
CLIENT: Irwin Union Bank

TMARKS DESIGN
803 S. KING ST.
SEATTLE, WA 98104
USA
206-628-6427
SUPERHERO@TMARKSDESIGN.COM
WWW.TMARKSDESIGN.COM

0426
ART DIRECTOR: Terry Marks
DESIGNER: Terry Marks, Kong Lu
CLIENT: TMARKS Design

0619
ART DIRECTOR: Terry Marks
DESIGNER: Terry Marks
CLIENT: Terry + Laura Marks

TOKY BRANDING + DESIGN
3001 LOCUST ST., 2ND FLOOR
ST. LOUIS, MO 63103
USA
314-534-2000
314-534-2001
WWW.TOKY.COM

0410
ART DIRECTOR: Eric Thoelke
DESIGNER: Katy Fischer
CLIENT: St. Louis Public Library
Foundation
WRITER: Geoff Story

0446
ART DIRECTOR: Eric Thoelke
DESIGNER: Mary Rosamund
CLIENT: St. Louis Public Library

0650, 0653
ART DIRECTOR: Eric Thoelke
DESIGNER: Jay David, Katy Fischer
CLIENT: Rebuilding Together - St.
Louis

0668
ART DIRECTOR: Eric Thoelke
DESIGNER: Mary Rosamond
CLIENT: The Unconscious

0910
ART DIRECTOR: Eric Thoelke
DESIGNER: Katy Fischer
CLIENT: Pulitzer Foundation for
the Arts

0913
ART DIRECTOR: Eric Thoelke
DESIGNER: Katy Fischer
CLIENT: Opera Theatre of St. Louis

0915
ART DIRECTOR: Eric Thoelke
DESIGNER: Katy Fischer
CLIENT: Susan and David Sherman

0987
ART DIRECTOR: Eric Thoelke
DESIGNER: Katy Fischer
CLIENT: Contemporary Art
Museum St. Louis

0997
ART DIRECTOR: Eric Thoelke
DESIGNER: Travis Brown
CLIENT: Food Outreach

1000
ART DIRECTOR: Eric Thoelke
DESIGNER: Mary Rosamund
CLIENT: St. Louis Public Library
Foundation

TOM, DICK & HARRY
ADVERTISING
4674 N. MANOR AVE., #3
CHICAGO, IL 60625
USA
773-756-8857
KIM@KIMKNOLL.COM
WWW.KIMKNOLL.COM

0591
ART DIRECTOR: David Yang
DESIGNER: Kim Knoll
CLIENT: The Korte Company

TOPOS GRAPHICS
55 SOUTH 3RD ST., 4TH FLOOR
BROOKLYN, NY 11211
USA
917-344-9834
SETH@TOPOSGRAPHICS.COM
WWW.TOPOSGRAPHICS.COM

0415
DESIGNER: Seth Labenz and
Roy Rub
CLIENT: Susan Engle

0457
DESIGNER: Seth Labenz and
Roy Rub
CLIENT: Columbus Bank and
Trust Co.

0467
DESIGNER: Seth Labenz and
Roy Rub
CLIENT: Topos Graphics

0609
ART DIRECTOR:
DESIGNER: Seth Labenz and
Roy Rub
CLIENT: Sima Familiant and
Sikkema Jenkins & Co.

UBER
ROYDS MILL, WINDSOR ST.
SHEFFIELD, YORKSHIRE S4 7WB
UK
0044 114 278 7100
AMY@UBERAGENCY.COM
WWW.UBERAGENCY.COM

0957, 0958
DESIGNER: Ricky Hewitt
CLIENT: BAFTA

UGLY DUCKLING PRESS
USA
ANDREW.M.GORIN@GMAIL.COM

0921, 0923
ART DIRECTOR: Andrew Gorin

UNDERLINE STUDIO
26 JOHN ST., SUITE 204
TORONTO, ON
CANADA
416-341-0475
FIDEL@UNDERLINESTUDIO.COM
WWW.UNDERLINESTUDIO.COM

0575
ART DIRECTOR: Fidel Pena, Claire
Dawson
DESIGNER: Emily Tu
CLIENT: Ben Weeks

VIÑAS DESIGN
67 VESTRY ST. NO. 8B
NEW YORK, NY 10013
USA
212-473-3471
JAIME@VINASDESIGN.COM
WWW.VINASDESIGN.COM

0627, 0977
ART DIRECTOR: Jaime Viñas
DESIGNER: Jaime Viñas
CLIENT: West/Keeler

0865
ART DIRECTOR: Jaime Viñas
DESIGNER: Jaime Viñas
CLIENT: Paige West

WALLACE CHURCH, INC.
330 EAST 48TH ST.
NEW YORK, NY 10017
USA
212-755-2903
CALLEY@WALLACECHURCH.COM
WWW.WALLACECHURCH.COM

0947
ART DIRECTOR: Stan Church
DESIGNER: Stan Church
CLIENT: Wallace Church, Inc.

0979
ART DIRECTOR: Stan Church
DESIGNER: Tiphaine Guillemet
CLIENT: Wallace Church, Inc.

0985
ART DIRECTOR: Stan Church
DESIGNER: Tiphaine Guillemet,
Bella Reiter, Kim Young

WARPEDESIGN
456 PROSPECT AVE., #2R
BROOKLYN, NY 11215
USA
718-809-9077
LUISESTROMBERG@YAHOO.COM
WWW.WARPEDESIGN.ETSY.COM

0130, 0134, 0135
DESIGNER: Luise Stromberg

WE ARE MESSENGERS
4/81 RICHMOND RD.
MORNINGSIDE, BRISBANE,
QUEENSLAND 4170
AUSTRALIA
61 7 3899 0045
TANYA@WEAREMESSENGERS.COM
WWW.WEAREMESSENGERS.COM

0145 – 0148, 0460
DESIGNER: Tanya Ruxton

WHIGBY
99 CROWN'S LANE, 5TH FLOOR
TORONTO, ONTARIO M5R 3P4
CANADA
416-923-6326
TODD@WHIGBY.COM
WWW.WHIGBY.COM

**0251, 0252, 0255 – 0262, 0267,
0268**
DESIGNER: Frank Viva
CLIENT: Whigby

0254
DESIGNER: Stuart Brown
CLIENT: Whigby

0263 – 0266
DESIGNER: Serge Bloch
CLIENT: Whigby

0331 – 0333
DESIGNER: Todd Temporale
CLIENT: Whigby

WHITE RHINO
41 2ND AVE.
BURLINGTON, MA 01803
USA
781-270-4545
JON@WHITERHINO.COM
WWW.WHITERHINO.COM

0429
ART DIRECTOR: Dan Greenwalk,
Kristen Cooper
DESIGNER: Jon Lopkin
CLIENT: White Rhino

WING CHAN DESIGN, INC.
167 PERRY ST., SUITE 5C
NEW YORK, NY 10014
USA
212-727-9109
WING@WINGCHANDESIGN.COM
WWW.WINGCHANDESIGN.COM

0456
ART DIRECTOR: Wing Chan
DESIGNER: Lang Xiao
CLIENT: American Express Bank

0461
ART DIRECTOR: Wing Chan
DESIGNER: Lang Xiao
CLIENT: The Standard Chartered
Private Bank

WINKBOX.COM
511 N. GROVE ST.
LINCOLNTON, NC 28092
USA
704-740-9676
EWA@WINKBOX.COM
WWW.WINKBOX.COM

0669
ART DIRECTOR: John Boatwright
DESIGNER: Ewa Powell
CLIENT: Winkbox

WONDER WONDER
132 JAVA ST., #1
BROOKLYN, NY 11222
USA
646-248-8870
HELLOHIKARU@GMAIL.COM
WWW.WONDERWONDER.INFO

0385
ART DIRECTOR: Hikaru Furuhashi
DESIGNER: Hikaru Furuhashi

WOO CHUNG STUDIO
45 RIVER DR. S.
JERSEY CITY, NJ 07310
USA
913-636-3677
WOO@FONZCROM.COM
WWW.FONZCROM.COM

0475
ART DIRECTOR: Woo Chung
DESIGNER: Woo Chung
CLIENT: Self

WORKTODATE
USA
717-683-5712
GREG@WORKTODATE.COM

0480
ART DIRECTOR: Greg Bennett
DESIGNER: Greg Bennett
CLIENT: Greg Bennett

YEE-HAW INDUSTRIES
PO BOX 6258
HOBOKEN, NJ 07030
USA
201-653-1063
INFO@JIMFLORA.COM
WWW.JIMFLORA.COM

0309 – 0316, 0710
ART DIRECTOR: Julie Belcher,
Irwin Chusid, Barbara Economon
DESIGNER: Julie Belcher, Irwin
Chusid, Barbara Economon
CLIENT: Jim Flora Art

YOUNG & RUBICAM
PALLADIOM BLDG., DUBAI MEDIA
CITY, 4TH FLOOR
DUBAI
UNITED ARAB EMIRATES
971 55 4974626
J.ALVARES@TEAMYR.COM

0548
ART DIRECTOR: Joseph Bihag
DESIGNER: Joseph Bihag
CLIENT: Asda'a PR Agency

0556
ART DIRECTOR: Richard
Gandiongco
DESIGNER: Richard Gandiongco
CLIENT: Young & Rubicam

ZEITHEIST PRODUCTIONS
19 DELEVAN ST., 45
BROOKLYN, NY 12231
USA
646-549-0333
JOSHUARAY@
LOSTPROPERTYINFORMATION.COM
WWW.THURSDAYCITY.COM

0598
ART DIRECTOR: Joshua Ray
Stephens
DESIGNER: Joshua Ray Stephens
CLIENT: Joshua Ray Stephens

0817
ART DIRECTOR: Joshua Ray
Stephens
DESIGNER: Joshua Ray Stephens
CLIENT: Mary Santanello &
Joshua Ray Stevens

ZINNOBERGRUEN GMBH
FÜRSTENWALL 79
40217 DÜSSELDORF
GERMANY
49 (0)211 99459495
OFFICE@ZINNOBERGRUEN.DE
WWW.ZINNOBERGRUEN.DE

0451
ART DIRECTOR: Bärbel Muhlack,
Tobias Schwarzer
DESIGNER: Bärbel Muhlack,
Tobias Schwarzer
CLIENT: Zinnobergruen GmbH

0573, 0976
ART DIRECTOR: Bärbel Muhlack,
Tobias Schwarzer
DESIGNER: Bärbel Muhlack,
Tobias Schwarzer
CLIENT: M-Real Zanders GmbH

ZYNC
282 RICHMOND ST. E., SUITE 200
TORONTO, ONTARIO M5A 1P4
CANADA
416-322-2865
AWARDS@ZYNC.CA
WWW.ZYNC.CA

0471
ART DIRECTOR: Marko Zonta
DESIGNER: Mike Kasperski, Clare
Chow
CLIENT: Zync

0504, 0989
ART DIRECTOR: Marko Zonta
DESIGNER: Mike Kasperski
CLIENT: Zync

MANY THANKS

To all the talented designers and illustrators, your
contributions to this book are greatly appreciated.

To the amazing A/M family, especially Kat, Jesse, Gus,
Jason, and Jenny for your tireless efforts in the creation
of this book.

ABOUT THE AUTHORS

Aesthetic Movement is a think tank for smart, creative
collaborations and a harbinger of style. We believe that
considered design and frequent brushes with beauty
can enhance the overall quality of life, and we aim to
contribute to that end with every project and partnership
we undertake. Our unique ability to provide award-winning
design services alongside our recognized sales and
marketing expertise enables us to present clients with the
most comprehensive solutions from concept to product to
market. Through the creation of relationships, products,
and environments, Aesthetic Movement endeavors to move
hearts and minds by advocating the extraordinary—not
proliferating the ordinary.